Imagery in Art and Literature

A Moss Family Publication

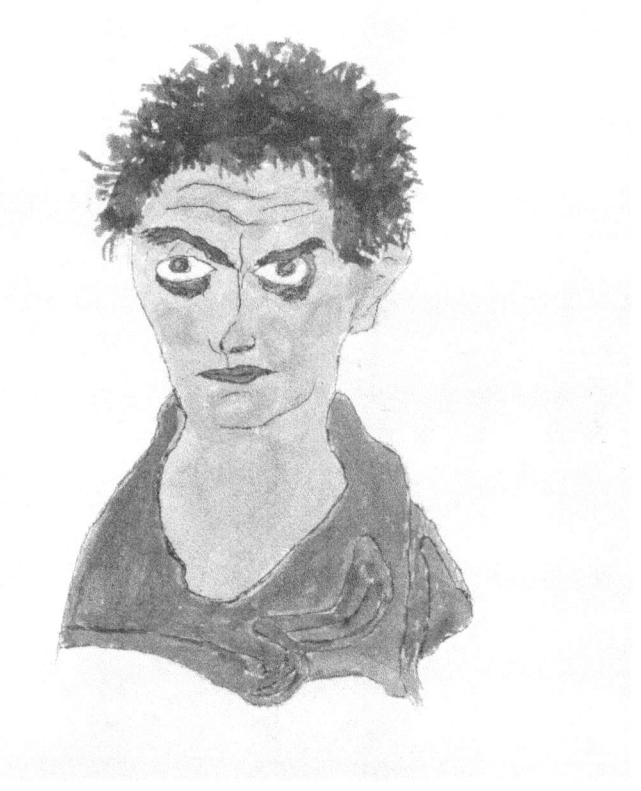

Egon Schiele, 1912 (copy)

Imagery in Art and Literature

Leonard Moss

Published by Moss Family Publications
http://mossfamilypublications.weebly.com/
Walnut Creek, California, 94595

Copyright © 2021 by Leonard Moss
All rights reserved
Imprint: Independently published posthumously
ISBN: 9798580140964
First edition: January 2021
Printed by Kindle Direct Publishing, an Amazon Company, U.S.A.
Available from Amazon.com

For Shaoping, Eli and Sara

"No, it is impossible, it is impossible to convey the life-sensation of any given epoch of one's existence—that which makes its truth, its meaning—its subtle and penetrating essence. It is impossible."

—Joseph Conrad, *Heart of Darkness*

ACKNOWLEDGMENTS

Again I am grateful to Shaoping for her love, care, and support.

Portions of this book were excerpted from three of my previously published books, The *Craft of* Conrad (Rowman & Littlefield, 2011), The *Tragic Paradox* (Rowman & Littlefield, 2012), and *Darwin, the Bible, and Tragedy* (Amazon KDP, 2019)

I have quoted lines or passages in the following works:

Primary Sources

The New English Bible, Oxford Study Edition, gen. ed. Samuel Sandmel (Oxford University Press and Cambridge University Press, 1961, 1970)

Eugene O'Neill, *Long Day's Journey into Night* (Yale University Press, 1956, 1962)

Samuel Beckett, *Waiting for Godot* (Grove Press, 1954, 1982)

William Shakespeare, *The Complete Pelican Shakespeare*, gen. ed. Alfred Harbage (Penguin, 1974)

Charles Darwin, *The Origin of Species*, 6th ed. (Penguin, 1958)

Joseph Conrad:

Conrad's "Heart of Darkness" and the Critics, ed. Bruce Harkness (Wadsworth, 1960)

Lord Jim, ed. Robert B. Heilman (Holt, Rinehart & Winston, 1957)

Nostromo, ed. Dorothy Van Ghent (Holt, Rinehart & Winston, 1961)

An Outcast of the Islands and Almayer's Folly, ed. Oliver Warner (Collins, 1955)

"The Shadow-Line" and Two Other Tales, ed. Morton Dauwen Zabel (Doubleday, 1959)

Tales of the East, ed. Morton Dauwen Zabel (Doubleday, 1961)

Tales of Heroes and History, ed. Morton Dauwen Zabel (Doubleday, 1960)

Three Great Tales (Random House, 1958)

"Youth" and Two Other Stories, ed. Morton Dauwen Zabel (Doubleday, 1959)

The Mirror of the Sea and A Personal Record, ed. Morton Dauwen Zabel (Doubleday, 1960)

The Complete Greek Tragedies, 4 vols., eds. David Grene and Richmond Lattimore (University of Chicago Press, 1959)

Nietzsche, Friedrich:
- *The Birth of Tragedy* and *The Genealogy of Morals*, trans. Francis Golffing (Doubleday, 1956)
- *The Complete Works of Friedrich Nietzsche*, ed. Oscar Levy, 18 vols (Macmillan, 1909-11, reprinted Russell and Russell, 1964)
- *Thus Spoke Zarathustra*, trans. Walter Kaufmann, *The Portable Nietzsche* (Viking, 1954)
- *The Will to Power*, trans. Walter Kaufmann and R. J. Hollingdale (Random House, 1967)
- Seneca, *Oedipus*, trans. E. F. Watling, *Seneca: Four Tragedies and Octavia* (Penguin, 1966)

Charles Baudelaire, "La Musique," trans. Francis Scarfe, in *Baudelaire (*Penguin, 1961)

Emily Dickinson, *The Complete Poems of Emily Dickinson,* ed. Thomas H. Johnson (Belknap Press of Harvard University Press, 1951, 1955, 1979, 1983)

Secondary Sources

Jane Kallir, *Egon Schiele* (Thames & Hudson, 2003)

Katie Hanson, *Klimt and Schiele Drawings* (MFA, 2018)

Jed Perl, "A Modernist Return to Reality," *New York Review*, Aug. 17, 2017

BOOKS BY LEONARD MOSS

—The key to vision is revision.

Arthur Miller (Twayne, 1967). Trans. Portuguese (Rio de Janeiro, 1968), Spanish (Buenos Aires, 1971), German (Darmstadt, 1972), Chinese (Beijing, 1987). 2nd ed., G.K. Hall, 1980. Paperback ed., G.K. Hall, 1984. Electronic ed., Gale, 2000

The Craft of Conrad (Rowman & Littlefield, Lexington Books, 2011)

The Tragic Paradox (Rowman & Littlefield, Lexington Books, 2012). Preliminary publication: *The Excess of Heroism in Tragic Drama* (University Press of Florida, 2000)

Along the Way: Owning an Identity, autobiography with Shaoping Moss (CreateSpace, 2017). Preliminary publication: *China Was Paradise! China Was Hell! (*XLibris, 2005*)*

Darwin, the Bible, and Tragedy (Amazon KDP, 2019). Preliminary publications: *The Evolutionary Sequence in Tragedy and the Bible* (Davies, 2008)

Darwin and Literature (Rowman & Littlefield, Lexington Books, 2014)

Darwin, the Bible, and Tragedy (Amazon CreateSpace, 2018)

Creating an Identity, with Shaoping Moss (Amazon KDP, 2020)

CONTENTS

Part I The Image in Fine Art

Chapter 1: Egon Schiele   3
    Definitions
    The Projection of Identity
Chapter 2: The Grotesque Self   17
Chapter 3: The Power of Intimacy   29
Chapter 4: High Spirits   39
Chapter 5: Faces of Children   47
Chapter 6: Faces of Age   53

Part II The Image in Literature

Chapter 7: Simplicity and Irony   59
    Hamlet and the Bible
    Irony in the *Oresteia*
    Seneca's Simplicity and the Eclipse of Light
    Nietzsche Explains Ambiguity
    Two Twentieth-Century Plays
Chapter 8: The Genius of Joseph Conrad   97
    A Master of Metaphor
    The Ethical Rivalry
    Darkness Versus Light
    The Dissolution of Identity
About the Author   151

Part I

The Image in Fine Art

1
Egon Schiele

Definitions

What is an image? Authors and painters combine two motives—to imagine a design and to fabricate a concrete rendition. Their creative imagination, the ability to visualize what is not visible, pictures the design mentally, than makes it tangible in the media of arts and crafts. A sensory or verbal medium may carry some particular meaning or emotional charge associated with the design; together they compose a metaphorical unit, an image.

An image is not merely a decoration or embellishment; imagery in fine art and literature configures identities, human or otherwise. And it can do far more than merely record faces and facts, or advance a craftsman's technical fluency. It can simplify, unify, fortify, color, and interpret concepts, intuitions, messages, or perspectives. It serves as an intermediary relating perception and intelligence to the outer world. While its primary purpose is to project identities, it can also transmit political, philosophical, subjective, or practical information.

Artists embody essential ideas in non-verbal media. Their images often imply meanings that cannot be made explicit; instead, the sensory surfaces appeal directly to the intellect, memory, and imagination without intercession by other media. A critical observer can estimate the effect of color, shading, and other properties, but the impact of a painting or drawing can only be suggested, not defined, by words.

Unlike the artistic image, a literary image presents a *verbal* representation. It appeals to sight and hearing through the symbolic medium of words rather than symbolic pictures. It can convey explicit as well as implied messages. In narrative and drama, with the connivance of rhetorical and metaphorical techniques, it often serves as a shifting battleground for moral contradictions, conversions, and "commingling."

A literary image is expressed in the unique idioms of a particular language by particular speakers at a particular period. It can convey one thing to one person, a contrary thing to another. Like an artistic image, it cannot be fully apprehended by any observer's translation. It too relies on the power of imagination to project identity.

What is a human identity? The sense of self is hard to define, a mysterious presence unique yet also generic. Far from being a stable commodity, it can be redesigned or renounced, corrupted or redeemed. Finality is problematic; our species seeks constancy but promotes variability.

An identity is extremely malleable. It can be fashioned in a huge variety of ways in response to particular challenges. As the situation demands, individuals can be quick-witted or deliberate, thoughtful or impulsive, continuous or fragmentary, derivative or unique, revolutionary or evolutionary, factual or visionary, honest or deceptive, predictable or idiosyncratic, rough or polished, youthful or mature, melodramatic or flat, simple or complex, verbose or succinct, comical or solemn.

It may be male oriented or female oriented, competitive or passive, intense or easygoing, dominant or subordinate, virginal or seasoned, diffuse or concentrated, temperate or radical, familiar (traditional, popular) or outlandish (innovative, strange), subtle (implicit) or obvious (explicit), useful or irrelevant, amateurish or sophisticated, cynical or optimistic, tense or relaxed, conclusive or tentative.

An identity can emphasize any of these attributes and exclude others, or oscillate between contraries, or reconcile the two sides of a contradiction. It is subject to a thousand influences and changes. It is a mutable commodity; the permutations are almost infinite (for further discussion, see my *Along the Way* and *Creating an Identity*).

The Projection of Identity

Egon Schiele, the well-known Austrian artist working at the start of the twentieth century, represented a variety of those permutations in his portraits and figure studies. Before his lamentable death at age 28 from Spanish flu in 1918, he produced some 2000 extremely proficient drawings and watercolors, in addition to dozens of oil paintings. His primary purpose was to picture the evolving facets of identity, whether stereotypical or eccentric.

To depict those facets, Schiele called upon three styles popular among creative artists at the time—realism, expressionism, and classicism, emphasizing one or the other at different times. He would portray a subject with realistic facts, or exaggerate it with expressionistic distortions, or dignify it with classical conventions, or immortalize it with a synthesis of the three styles.

The results were unique. He blended grotesque postures and facial poses with everyday appearances, scandalous exposures with traditional façades, delirious colors with common formulas, vibrant details with old-fashioned templates, tense muscle dispositions with careless body arrangements.

As Jane Kallir notes in *Egon Schiele,* his early self-portraits and female figures accentuated surreal distortions; later he focused on the actual features of individuals:

whereas most of Schiele's 1910 nudes . . . were notably lacking in personality, by the end of that year the artist had begun to evidence a far more intense emotional engagement with his models. . . . Loss of identity had threatened to engulf him.... The women in the [later] drawings are invariably alert, vibrant human beings with a palpable presence. Just as Schiele once boldly chronicled the power of female sexuality, he now acknowledged [specific] female identity.

In every style he worked hard to grasp a substantial personality, whether generalized (the female as sexual mechanism, the male as muscular model or unrestrained vagabond), or intimate and distinctive, or a brilliant amalgam of both. His watercolors are ironic, unpretentious, spontaneous, aflame with youthful energy. They deliver tentative, not definitive, appraisals in quick, piercing assessments. His principal purpose was to conceive and assert a creative self. "You must work to represent visually . . . your spiritual life, your worldview, and your impressions of life," he advised (quoted in Katie Hanson, *Klimt and Schiele Drawings*).

Had Schiele survived the Spanish flu, he might have gone further with the techniques he experimented with so energetically and so successfully. He might have shown in greater depth how twisted facial expressions and abnormal arrangements of heads, bodies, and limbs can indicate emotional or moral configurations.

Why use copies to demonstrate his talent rather than reproductions of the original works? Because trying to duplicate Schiele's colors and contours gives an amateur admirer greater access to the artist's imagination, a useful exercise. The self-portraits and figure studies are fairly easy to copy because they often feature stereotypical or contorted facial features and postures, highly animated and extravagant. On the other hand, they are hard to *imitate* because even the stereotypes or distortions transmit a strong sense of personality that most artists can only hint at.

This chapter offers a glimpse of Schiele's charm. The chapters following illustrate aspects of identity that have intrigued Schiele and others—grotesque fantasies, relationship perils and pleasures, vibrant vitality, childish innocence, and old-age decrepitude.

Imagery in Art and Literature

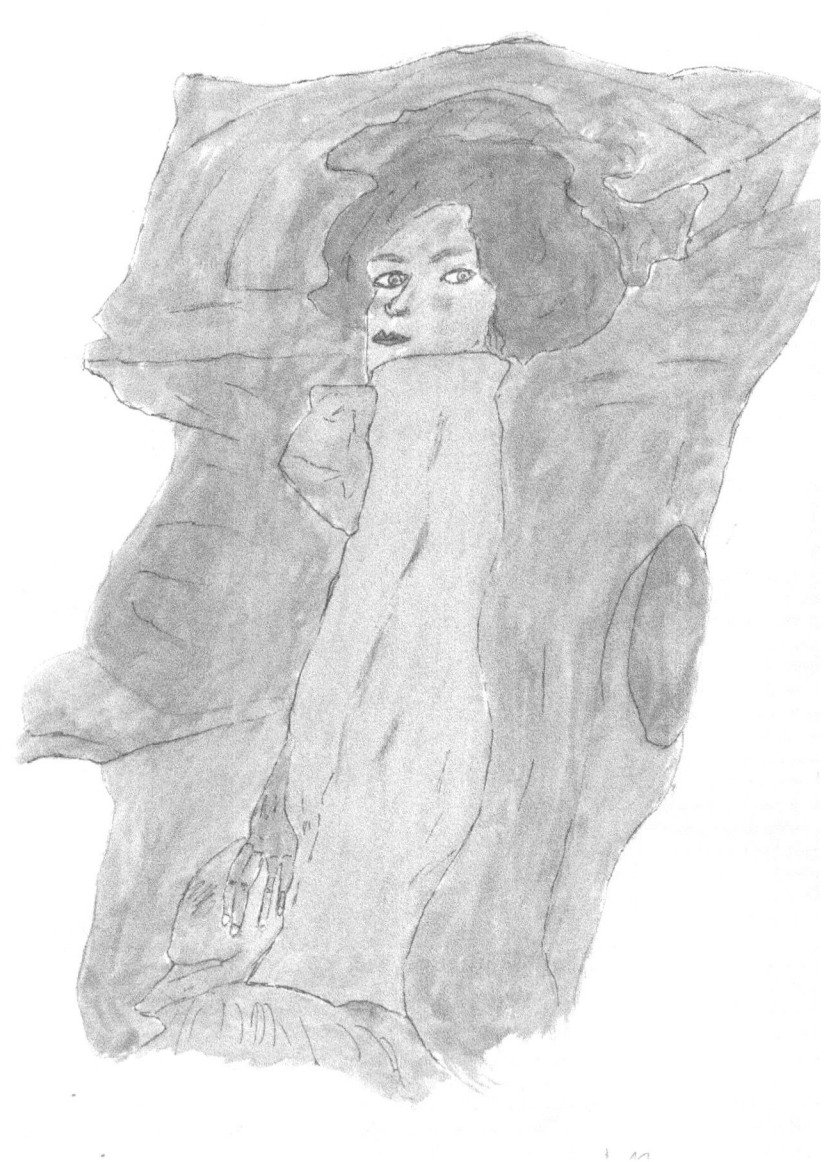

Egon Schiele, 1910

Egon Schiele

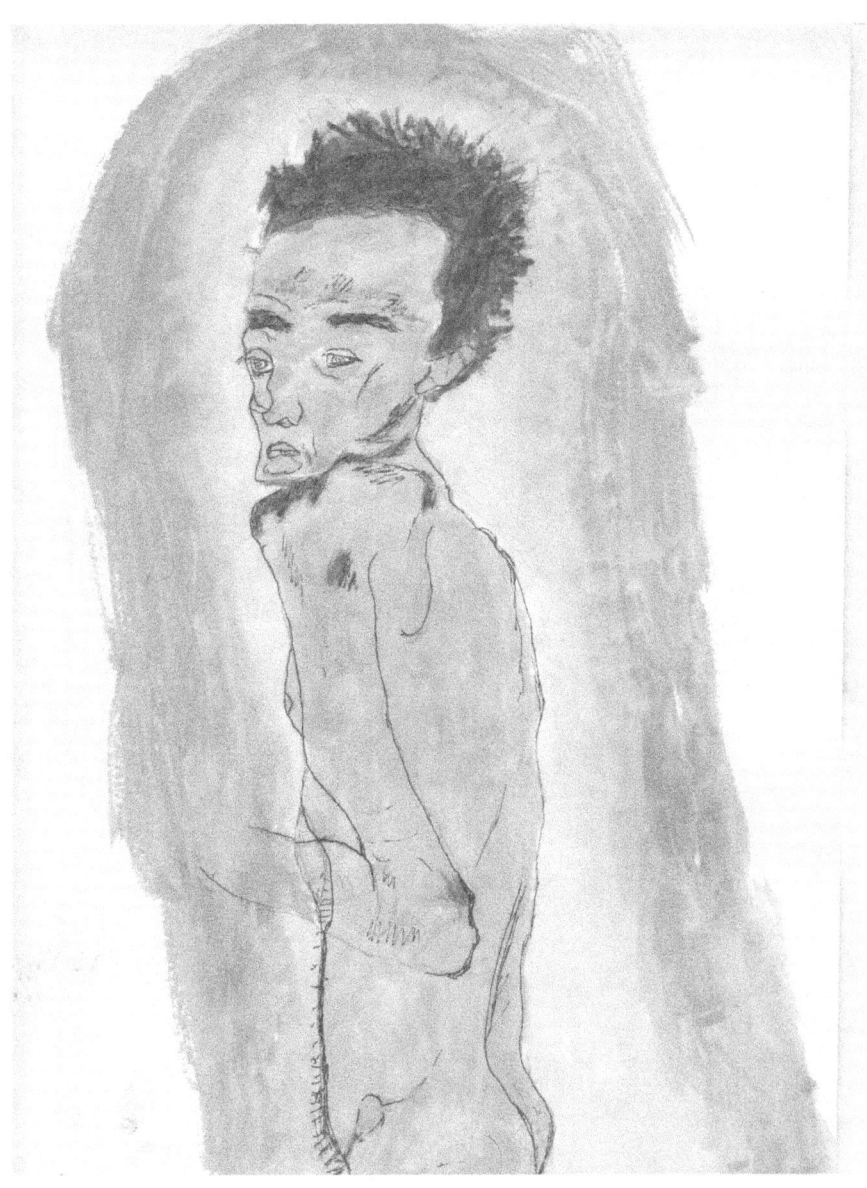

Egon Schiele, 1910

Imagery in Art and Literature

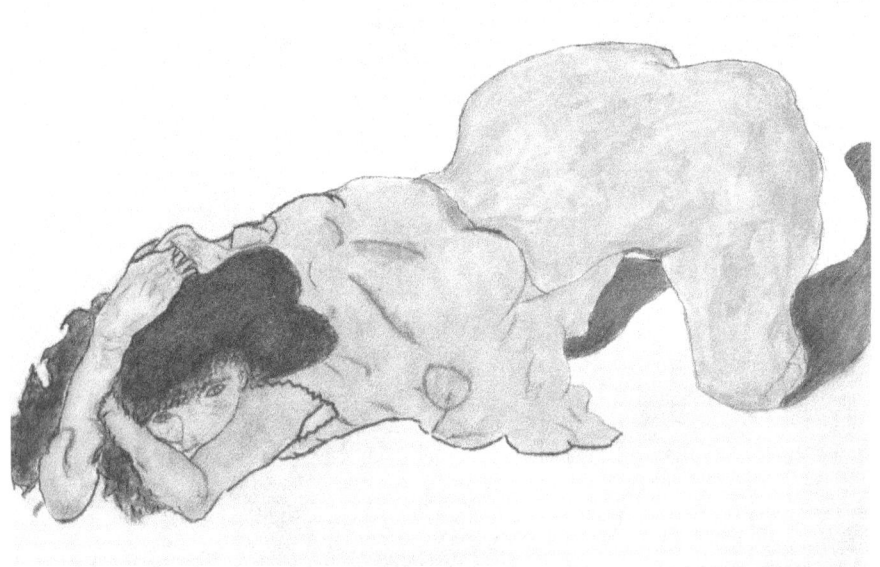

Egon Schiele, 1910

Egon Schiele

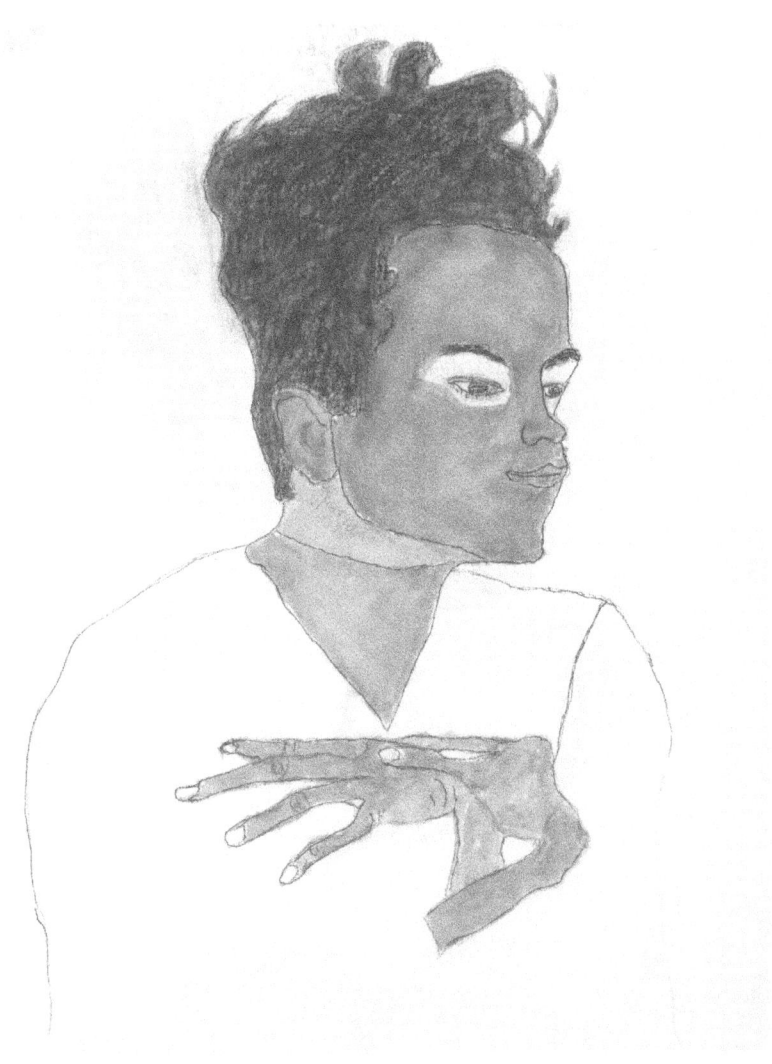

Egon Schiele, 1910

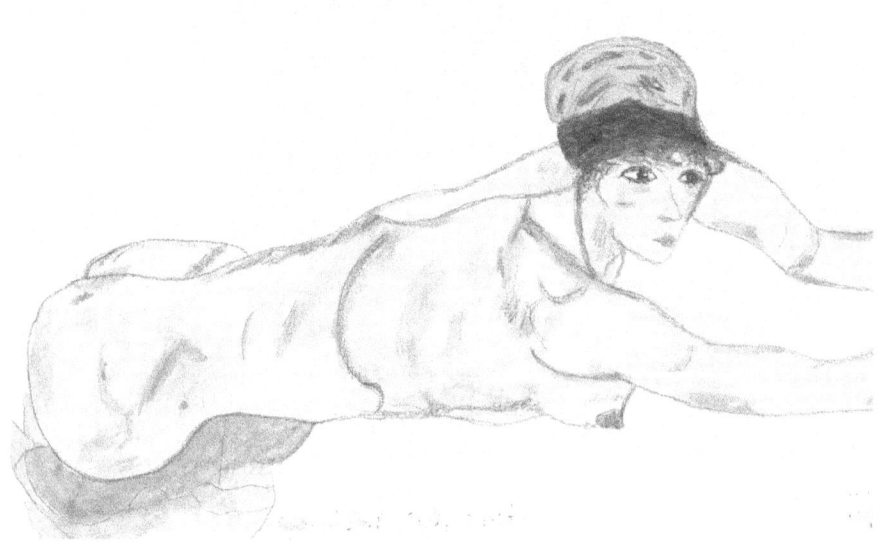

Egon Schiele, 1914

Egon Schiele

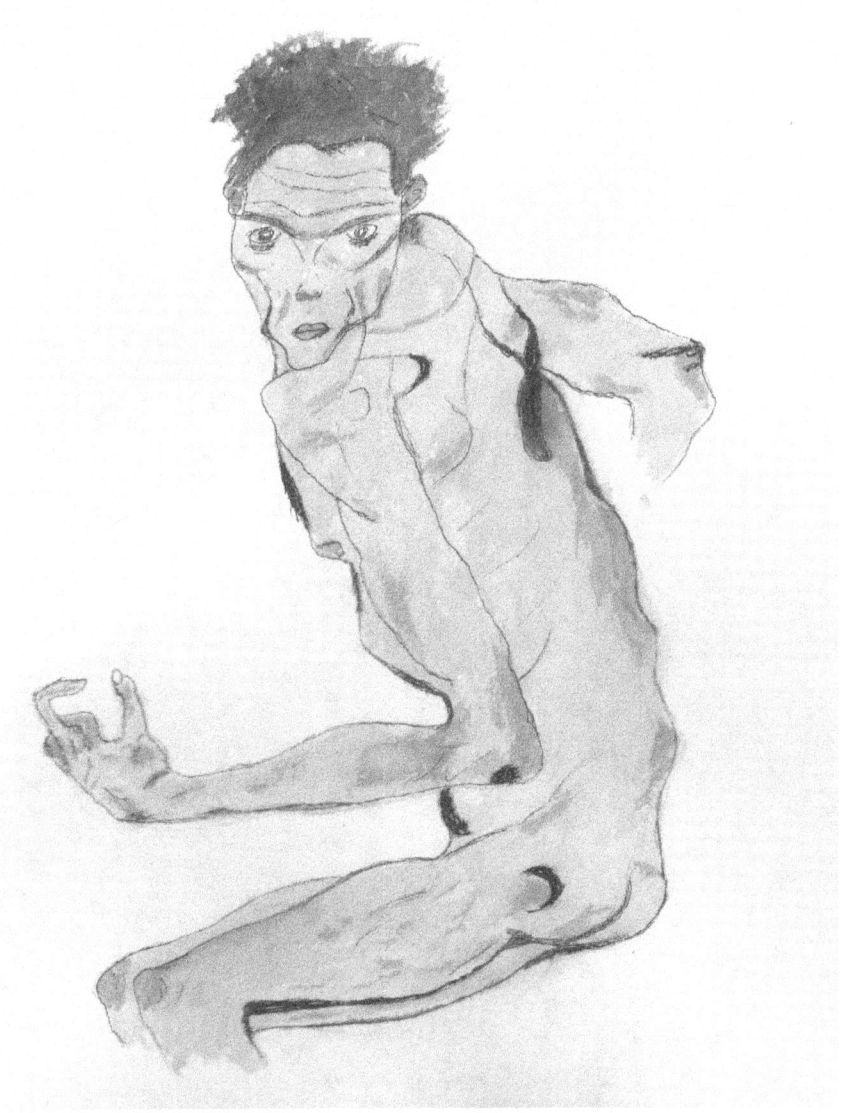

Egon Schiele, 1913

Imagery in Art and Literature

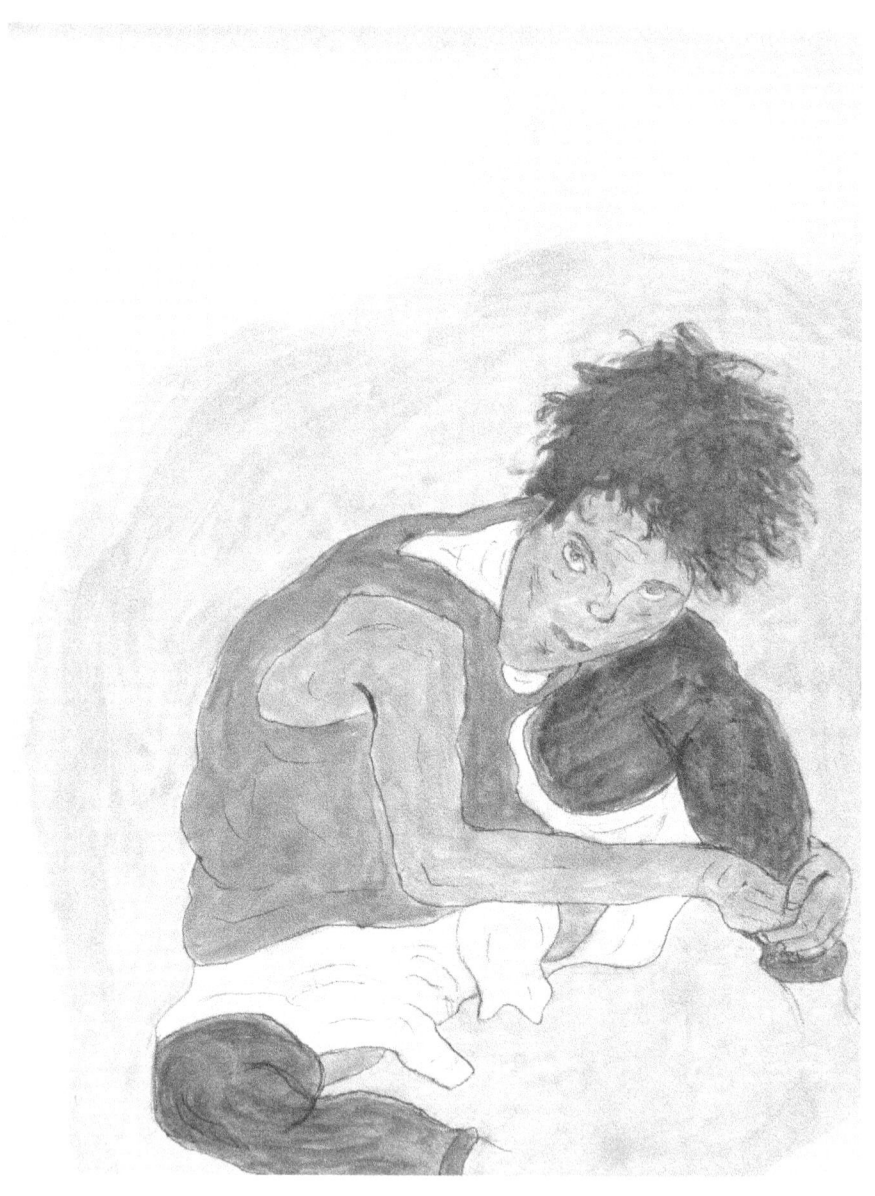

Egon Schiele, 1917

Egon Schiele

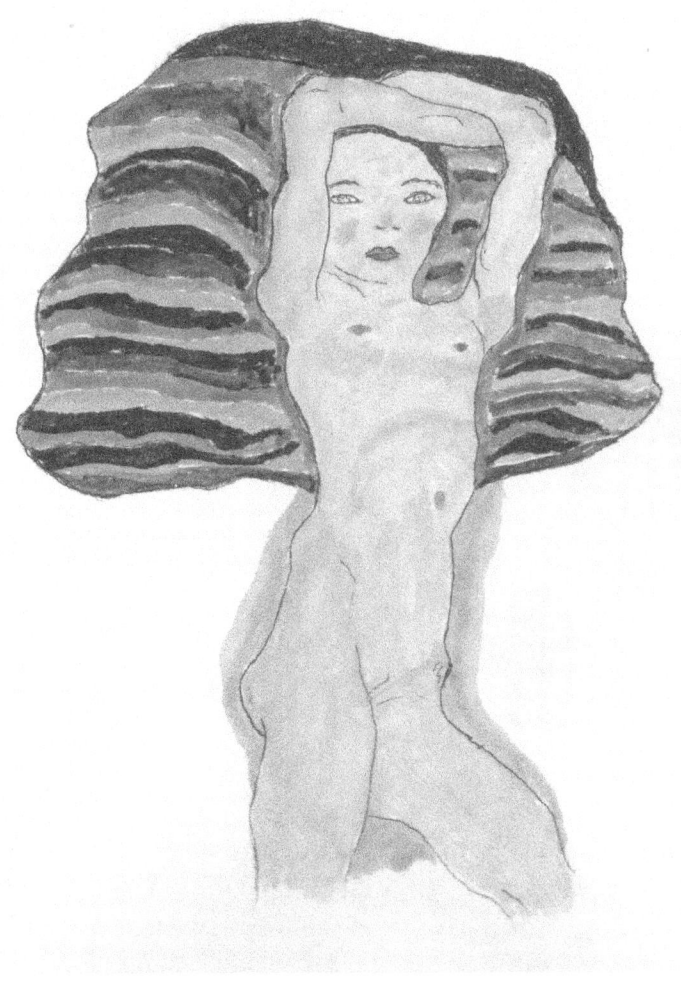

Egon Schiele, 1911

2
The Grotesque Self

Weird figures and faces can imply weird inward qualities. Schiele and other artists in the early twentieth-century experimented with a blend of factual realism, classical elegance, and subjective feelings. To integrate emotional dynamics with abstract concepts they exaggerated, distorted, and intensified physical features, postures, and colors.

A relevant statement on modern art by Jed Perl in "A Modernist Return to Reality," *New York Review*, Aug. 17, 2017, discusses images that escape the restrictions imposed by realistic (photographic) depiction:

> All these artists [Picasso, Matisse, Derain, Giacometti, Balthus], Derain as much as Picasso, embraced the fundamental modern discovery that the essence of the visual arts wasn't naturalistic truth but pictorial truth. A work of art was first and foremost an arrangement of forms, which had both emotional and symbolic implications.
>
> With Picasso and Matisse, the constant rearrangement of forms became a way of generating emotions and symbols that reflected the artist's kaleidoscopic personality. [But] Derain, Giacometti, and Balthus were troubled by what they saw as the subjectivity of such constantly mutating forms. While they were too thoroughly modern to revert to the old

idea that a painting was a mirror of the visible world, they wanted their imaginary worlds to have a logic and inevitability that transcended their own emotional appetites.

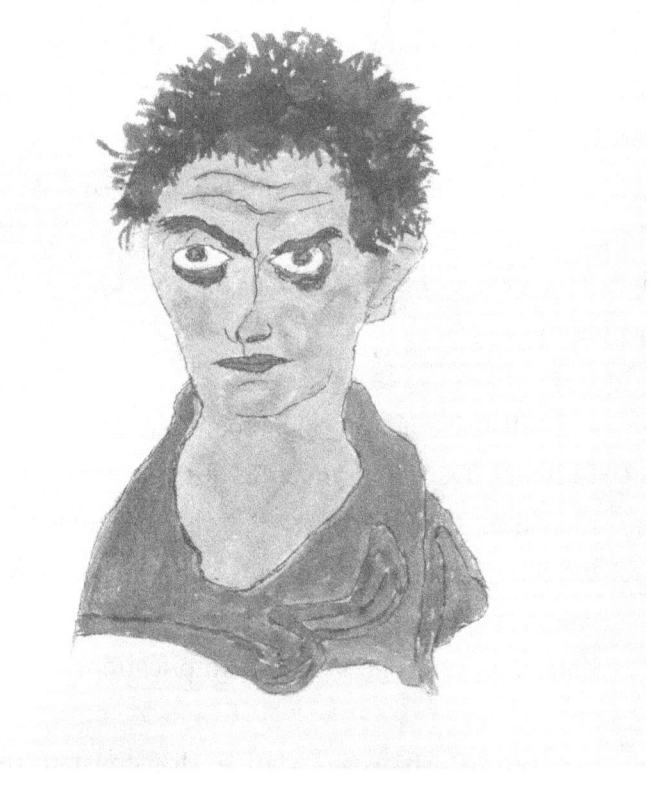

Egon Schiele, 1912

The Grotesque Self

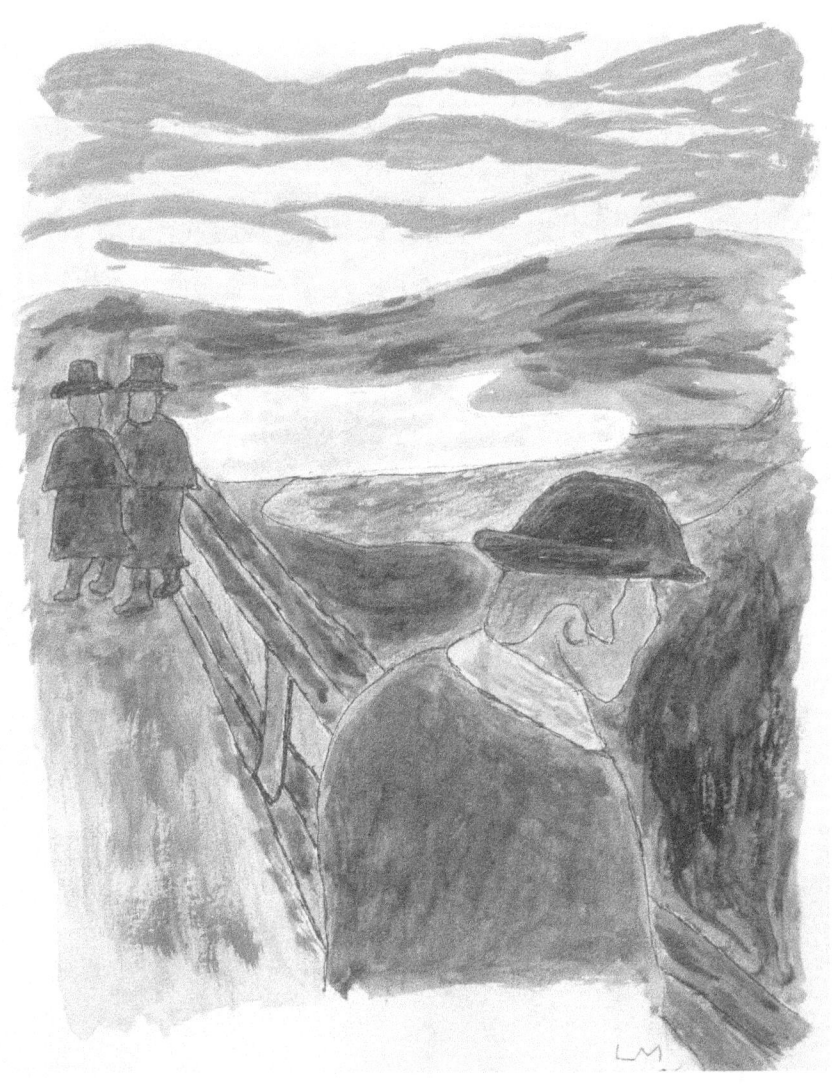

Edvard Munch, 1892

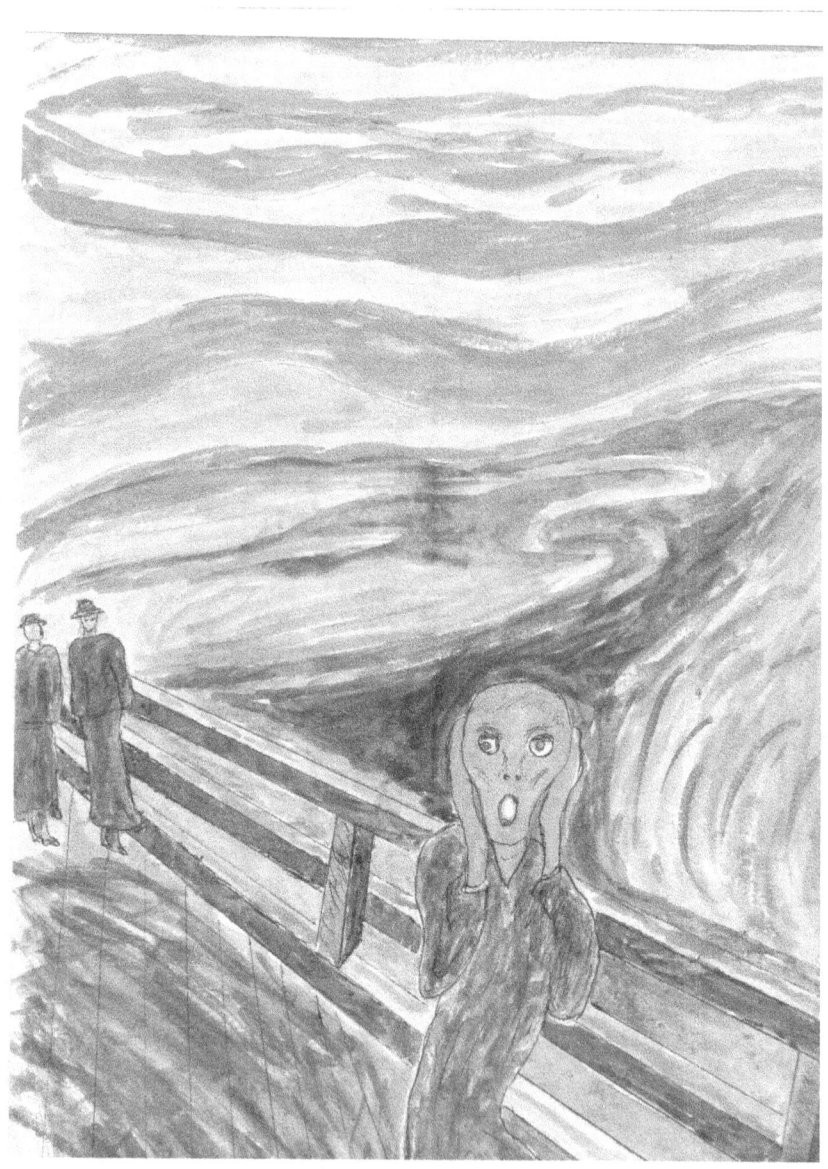

Edvard Munch, 1893

The Grotesque Self

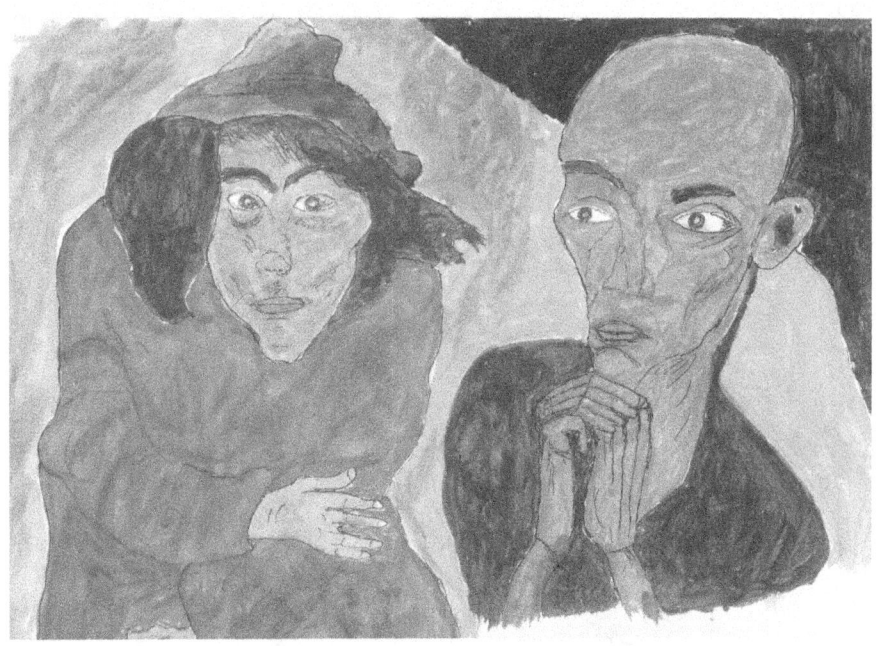

Chaim Soutine, 1920   Erich Heckel, 1919

Imagery in Art and Literature

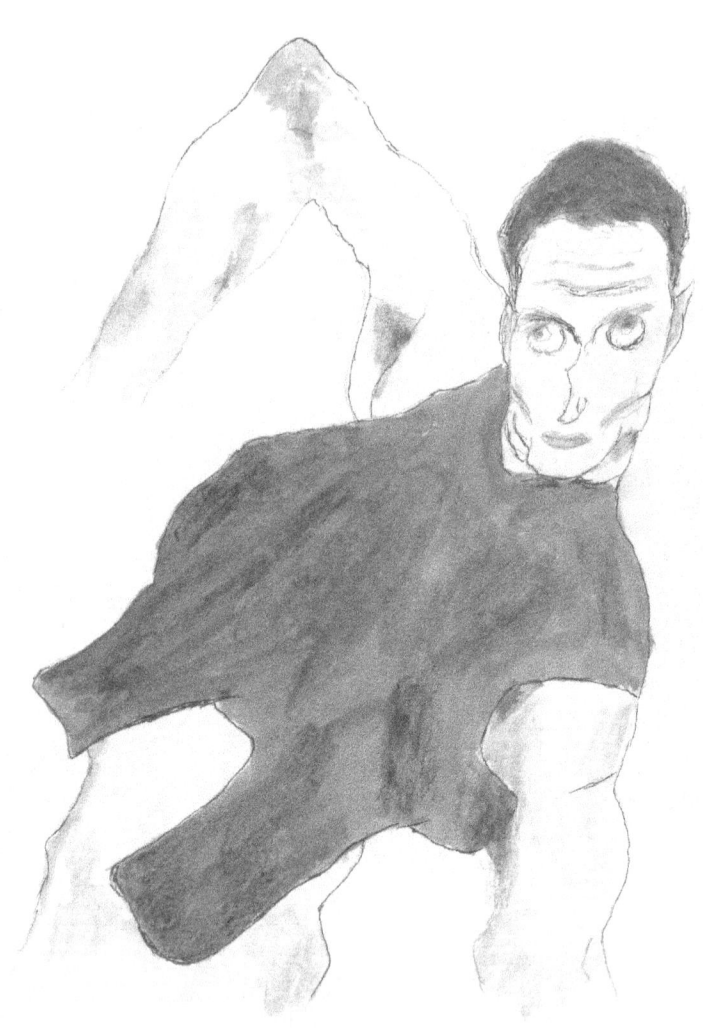

Egon Schiele, 1914

The Grotesque Self

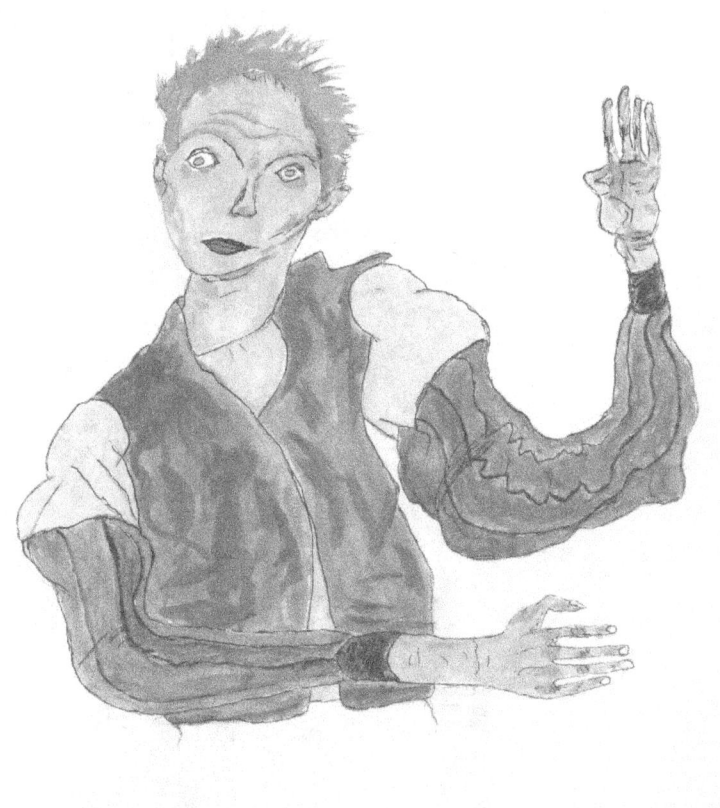

Egon Schiele, 1915

Imagery in Art and Literature

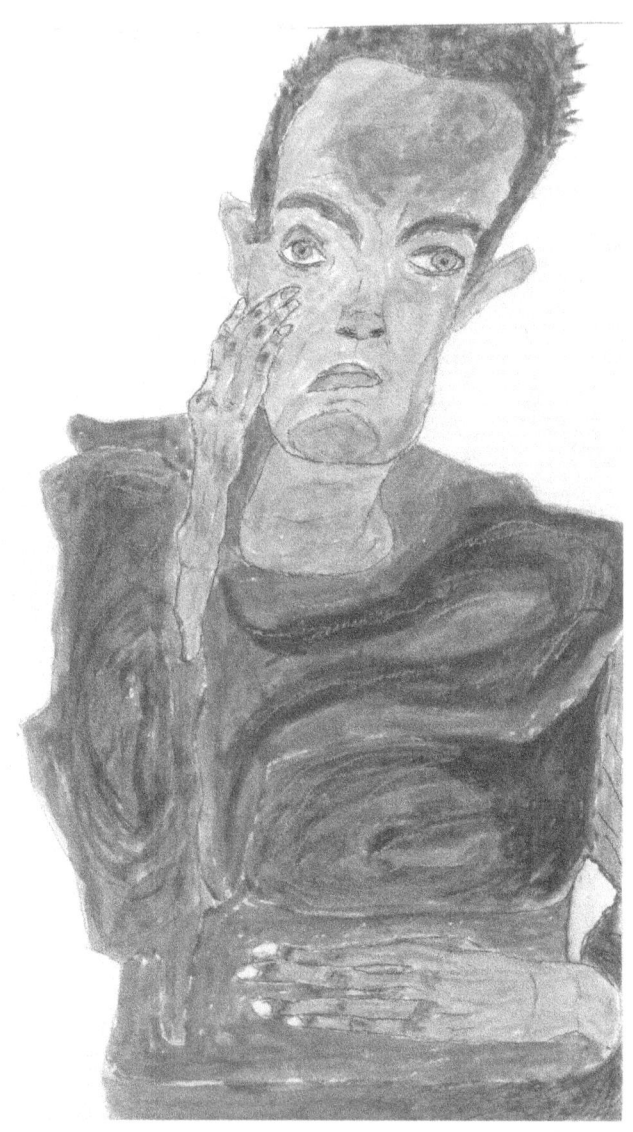

Egon Schiele, 1910

The Grotesque Self

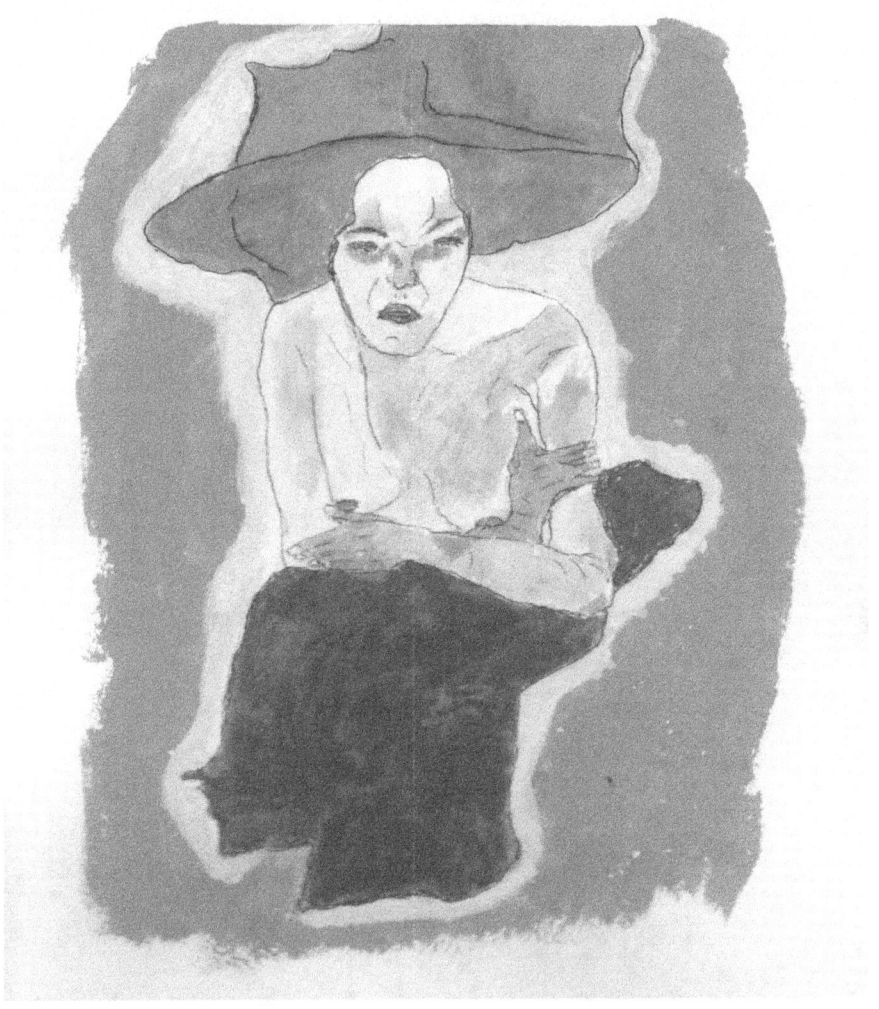

Egon Schiele, 1910

Imagery in Art and Literature

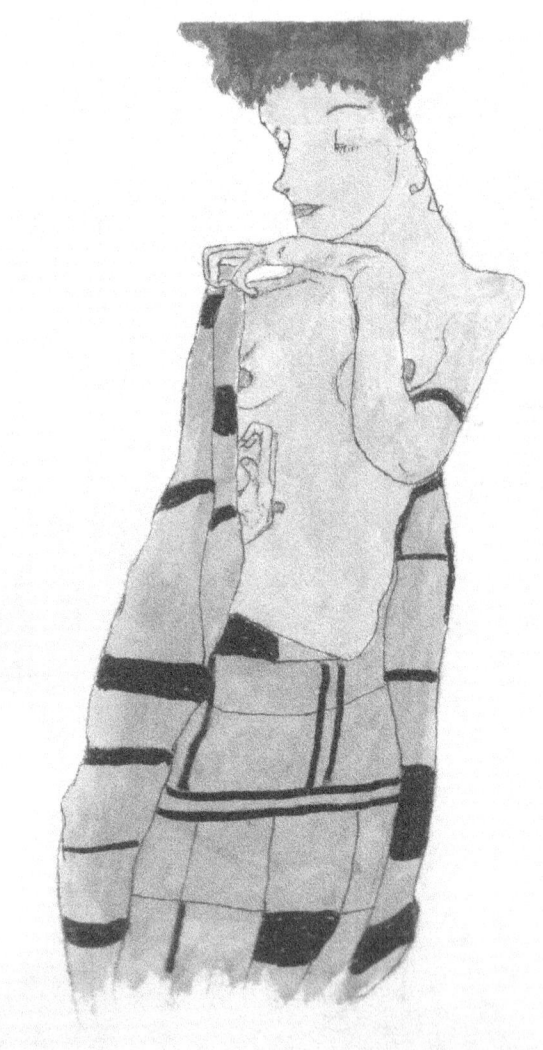

Egon Schiele, 1910

The Grotesque Self

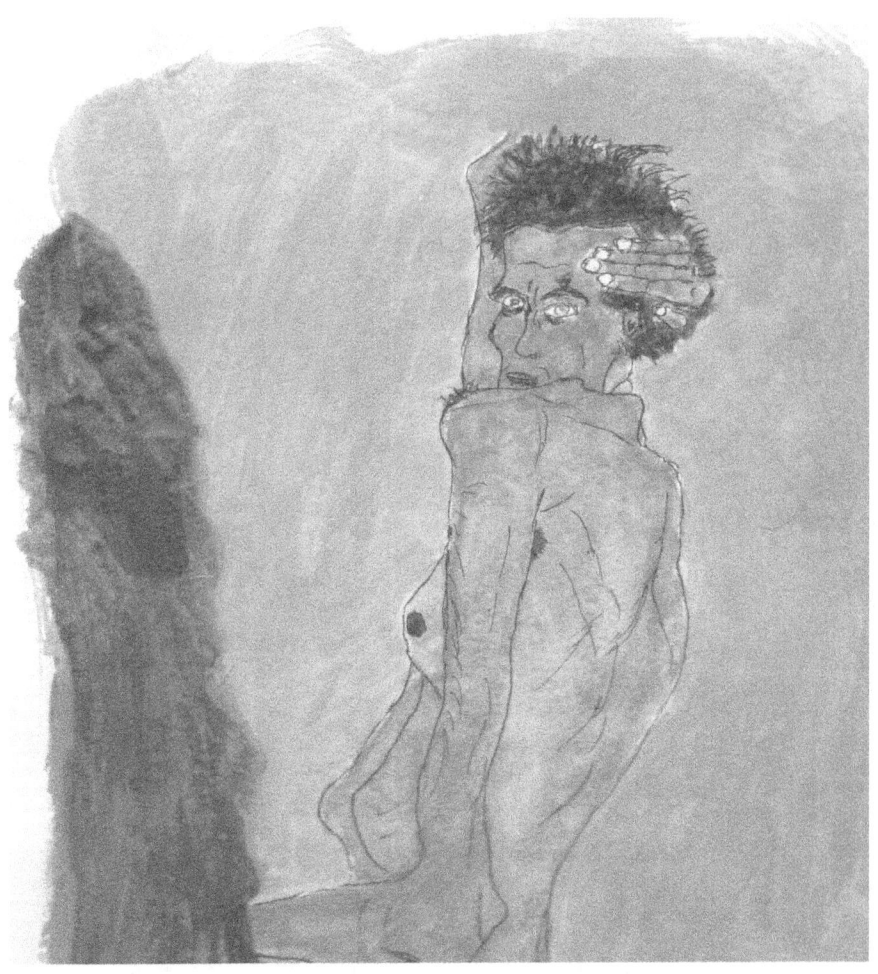

Egon Schiele, 1910

3
The Power of Intimacy

Artists have been concerned to show the appearance of both intimacy and its failure, but they find it difficult to depict human relationships, happy or otherwise. They cannot dramatize, as playwrights and other literary craftsmen can, interaction between individuals. They must *imply* psychological or spiritual interaction through facial features, bodily postures, and other visible signs. To a selection of copies that illustrate those signs, I add several of my homemade images drawn from magazine photos.

Imagery in Art and Literature

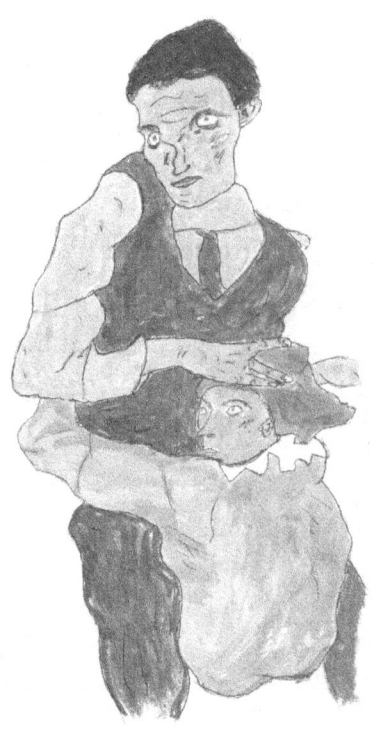

Egon Schiele, 1915

The Power of Intimacy

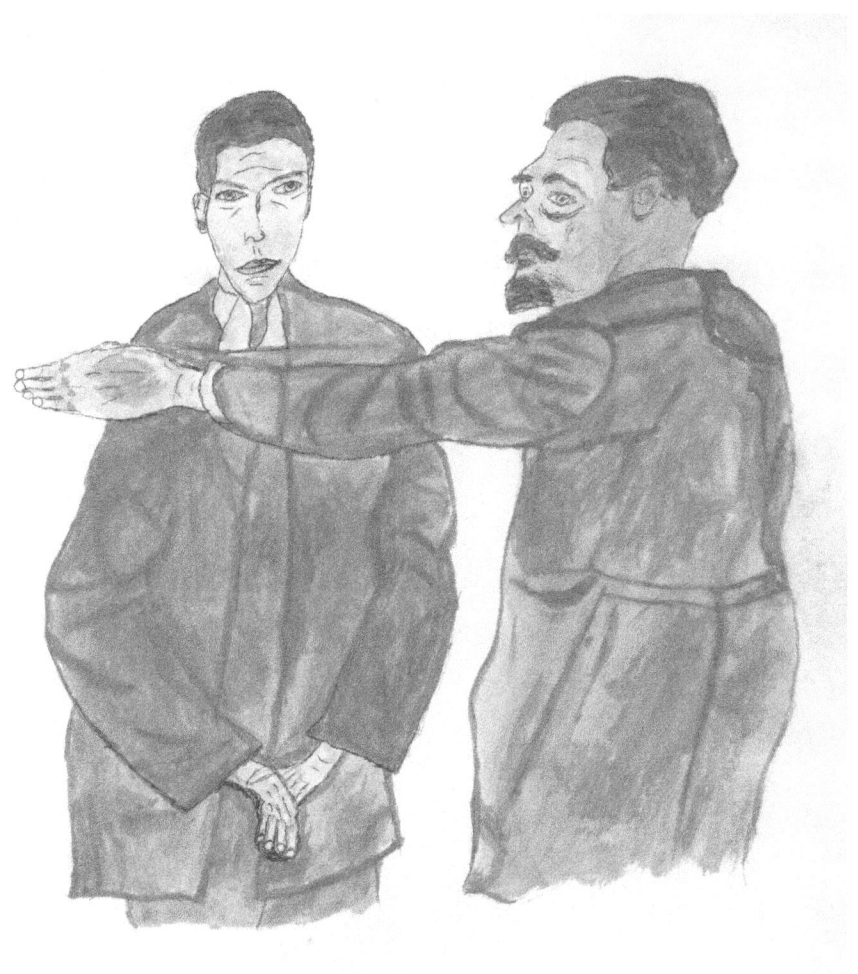

Egon Schiele, 1913

Imagery in Art and Literature

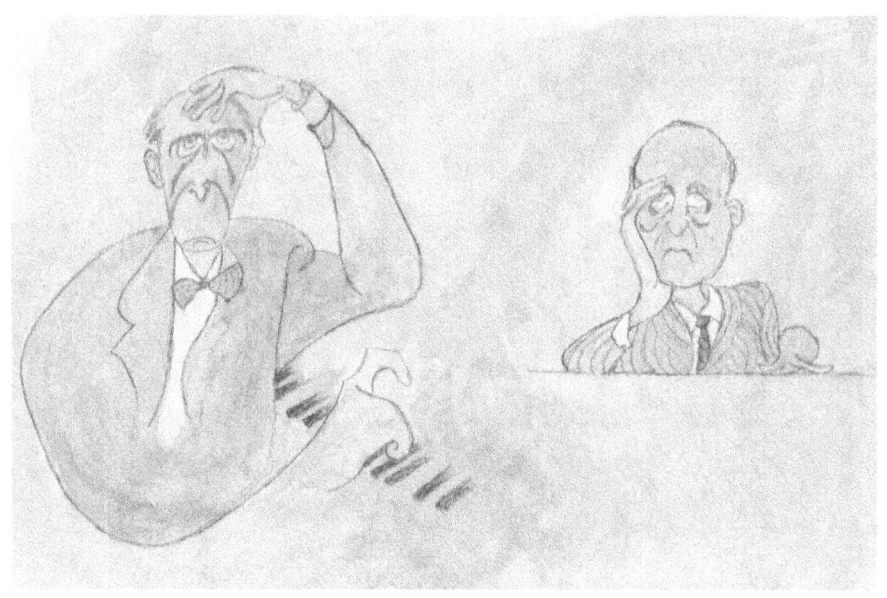

Al Hirschfeld, 1981

The Power of Intimacy

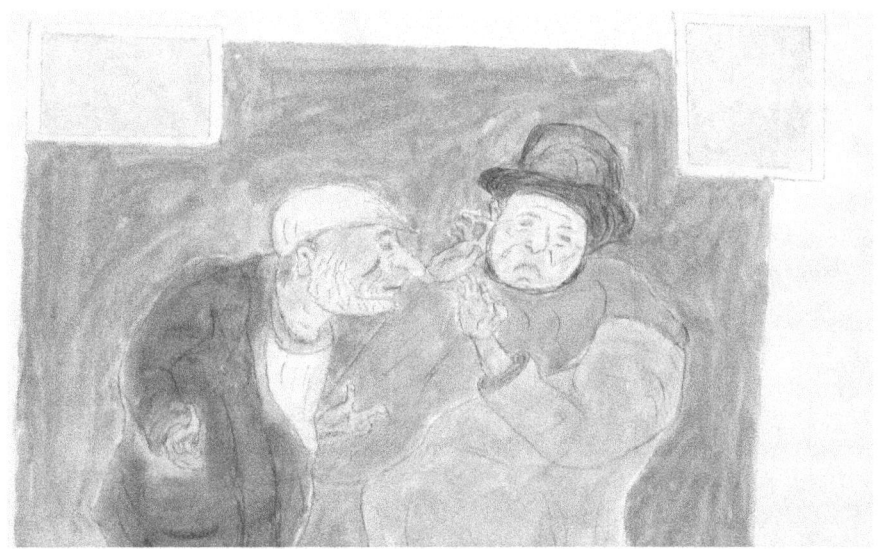

A. Reynard, 1930s

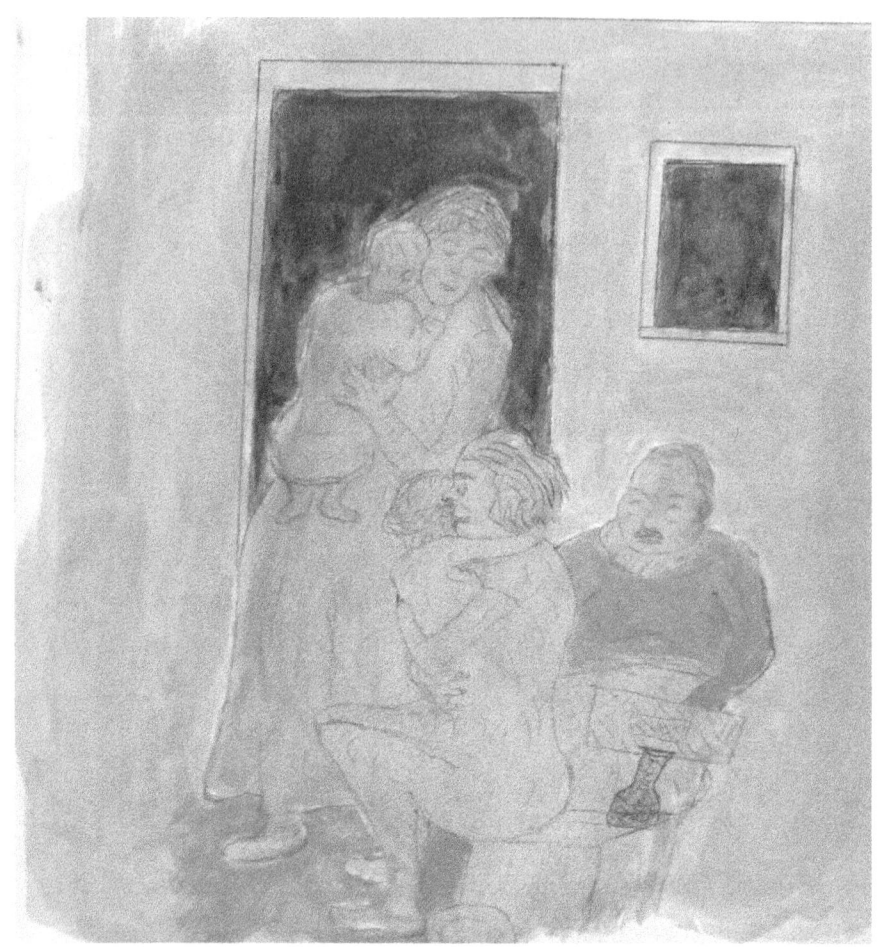

A. Reynard, 1930s

The Power of Intimacy

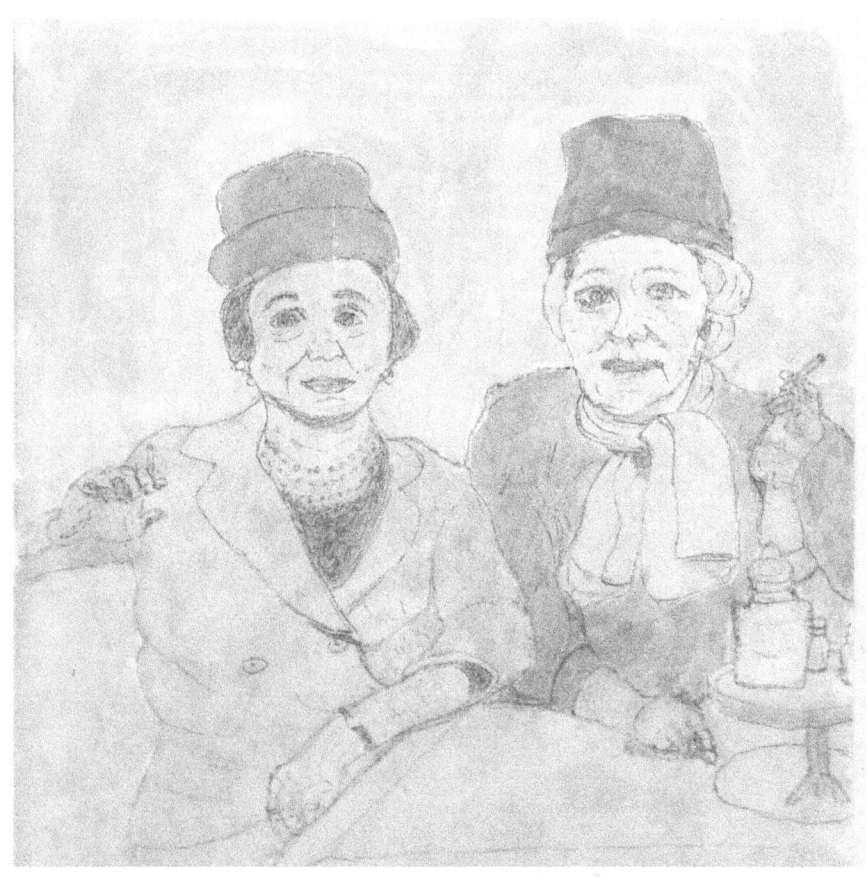

Len Moss, 2017

Imagery in Art and Literature

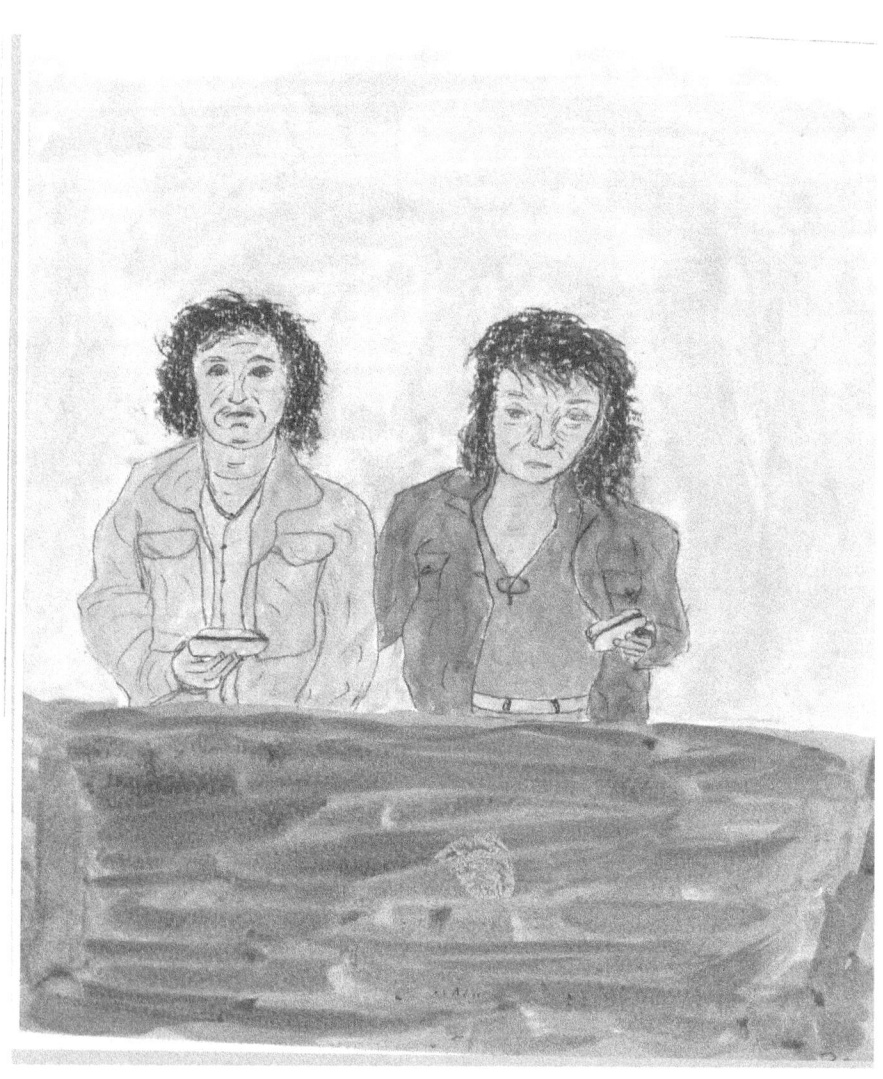

Len Moss, 2018

The Power of Intimacy

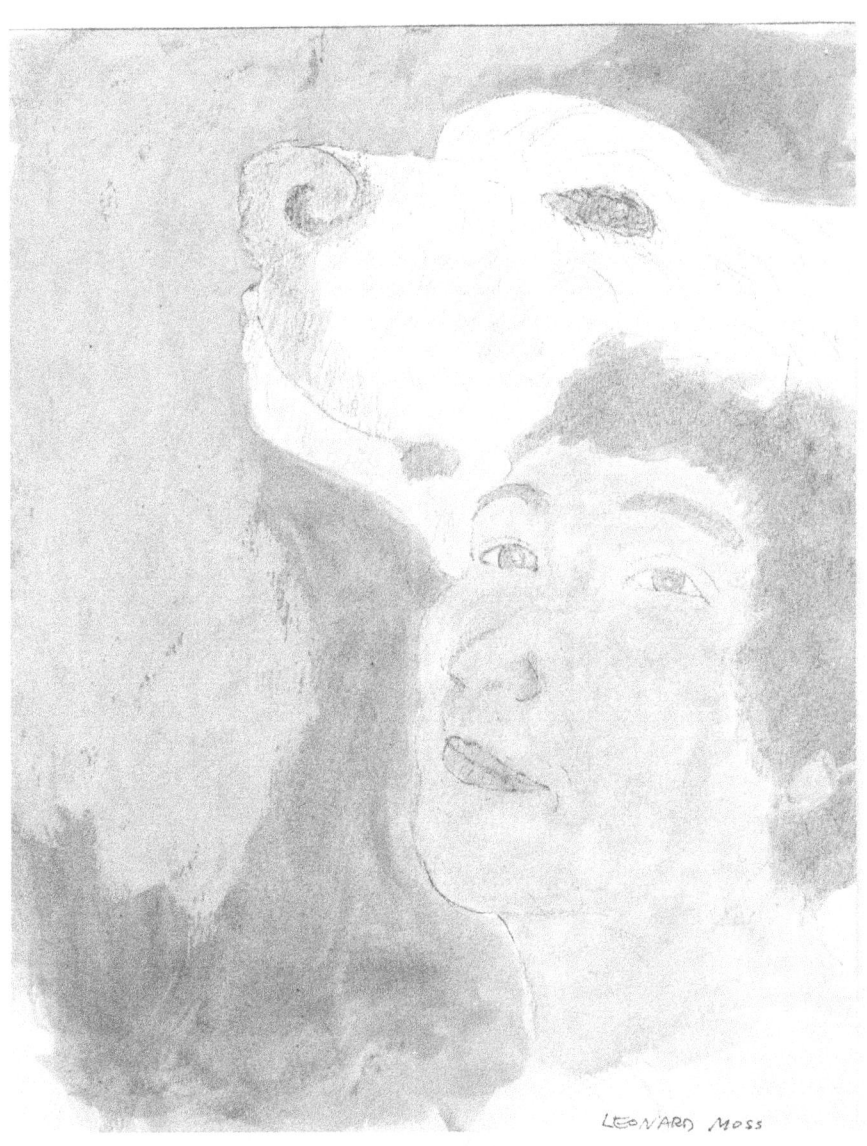

Len Moss, 2017

Imagery in Art and Literature

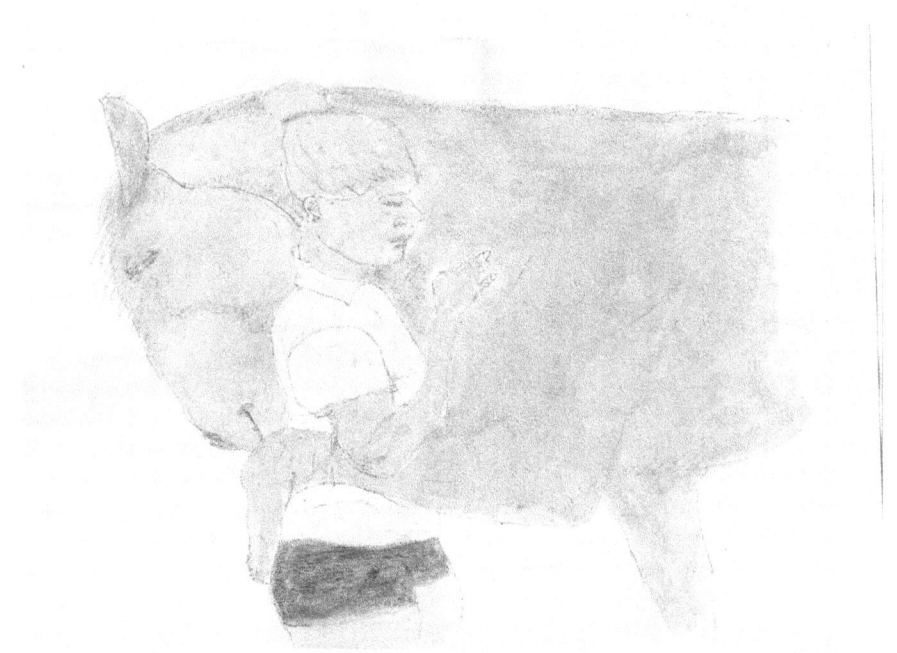

Len Moss, 2017

4
High Spirits

Some artists have focused on the blossoming of vitality. A painter can, like a good actor, create the appearance (or illusion) of resilience, buoyancy, good health, affirmative outlook, and vibrant energy. He can depict robust figures working and playing, raising children, singing and dancing, emanating love and good will, celebrating their lives, not only surviving but *delighting* in survival. They enjoy. They smile.

Al Hirschfeld exhibited that exuberance in countless high-spirited, good-natured caricatures of celebrities in sports, show business, and politics. Here are samples of his drawings, along with two of my own designs:

Imagery in Art and Literature

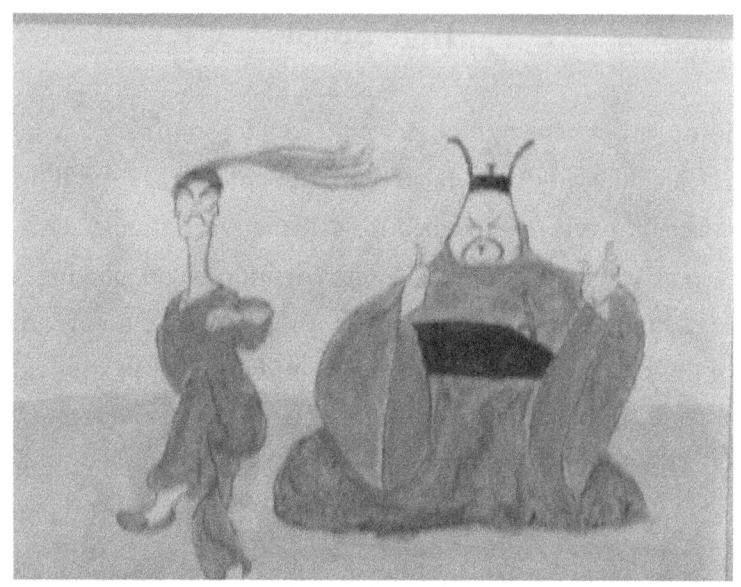

Al Hirschfeld, 1981, 1985

High Spirits

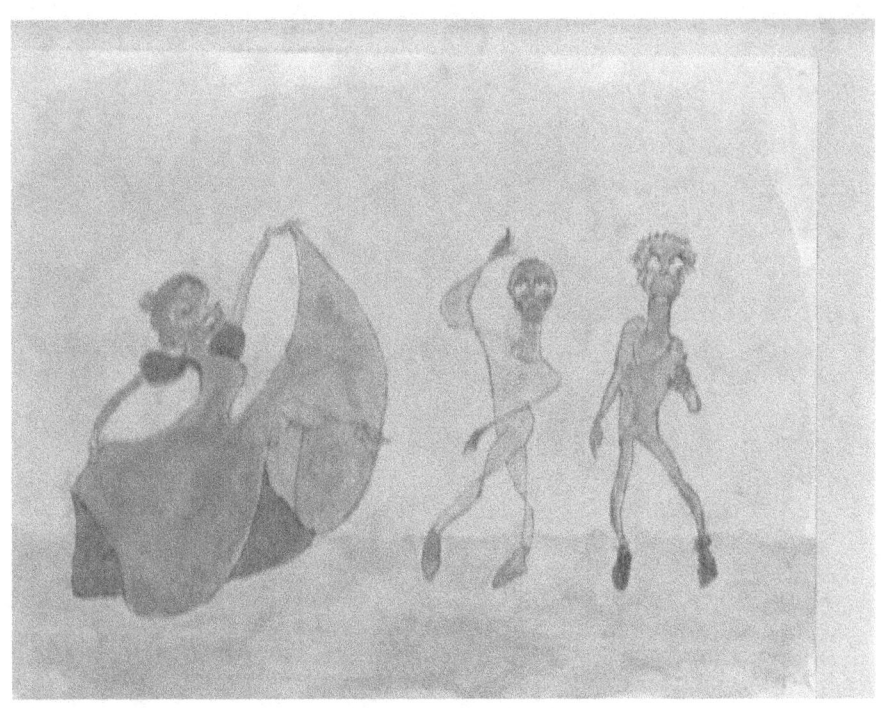

Al Hirschfeld, 1937, 2001

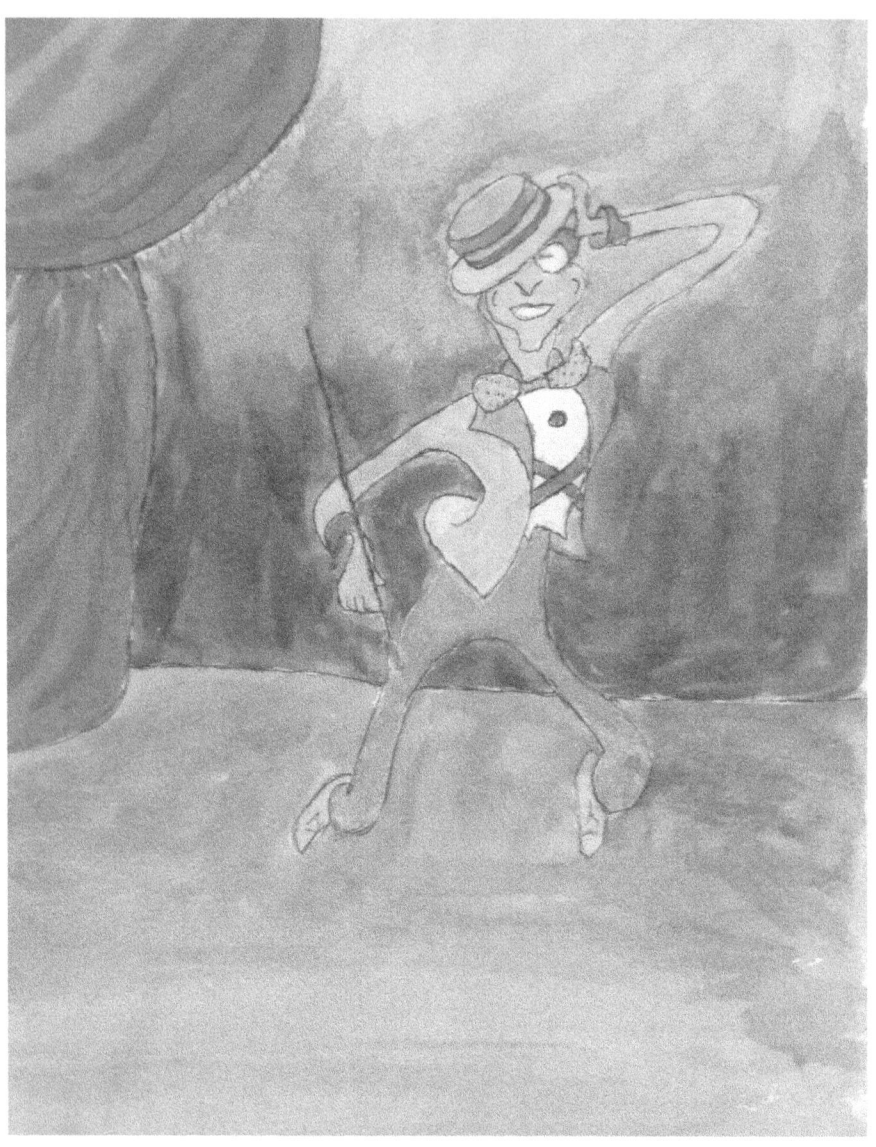

Al Hirschfeld, 2000

High Spirits

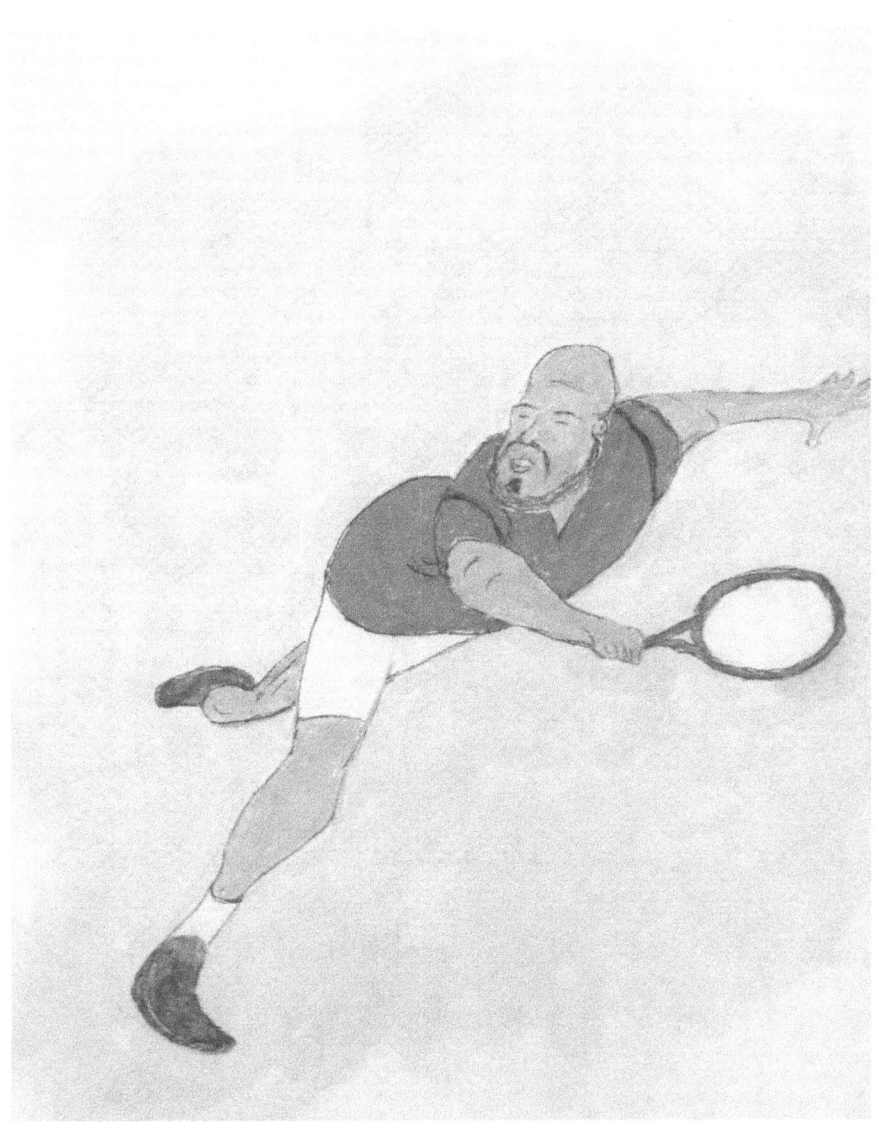

Al Hirschfeld, 2000

Imagery in Art and Literature

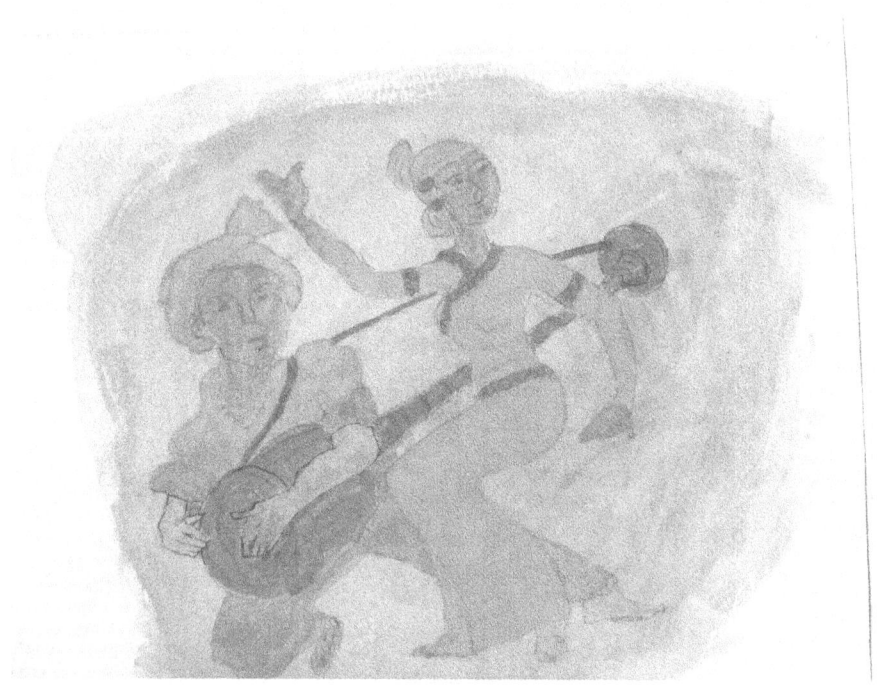

Len Moss, 2017

High Spirits

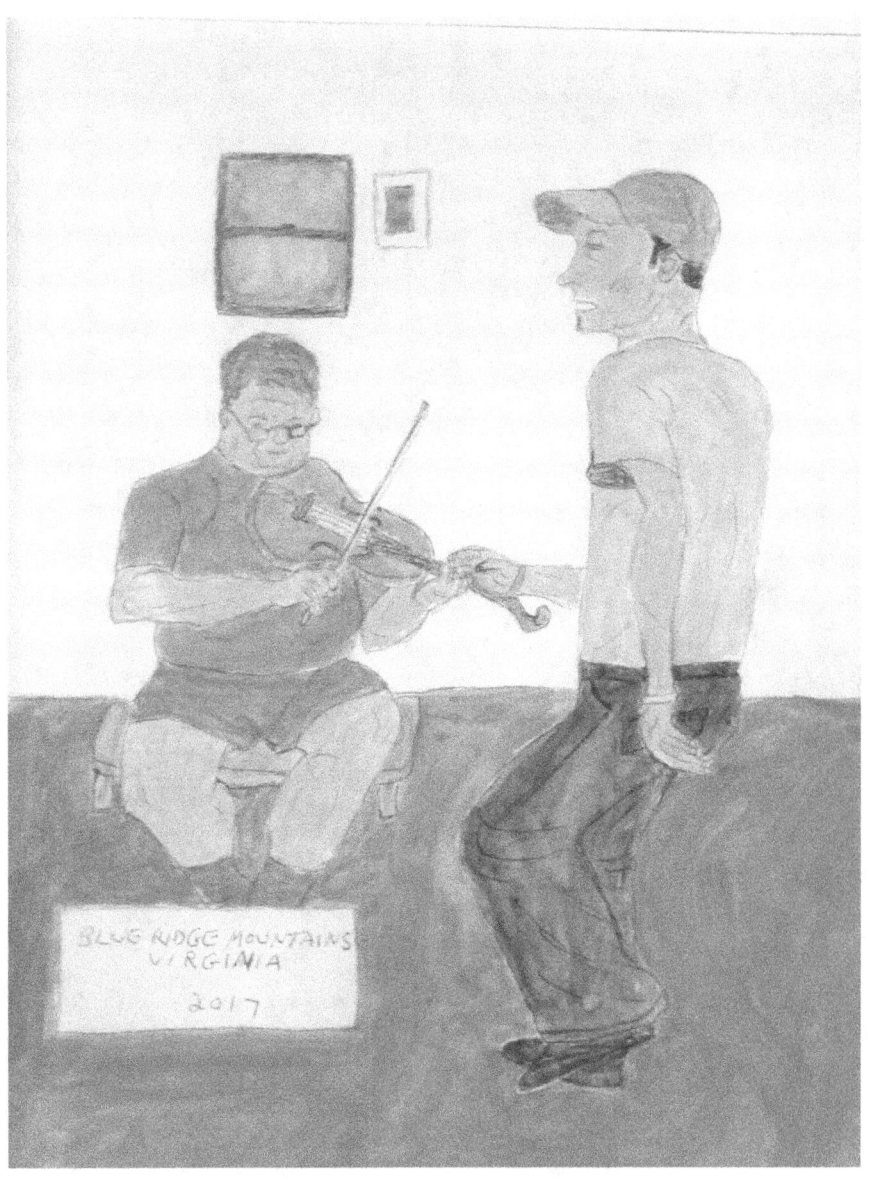

Len Moss, 2017

5
Faces of Children

In contrast to a few animated children, most youngsters in Schiele's drawings seem strangely impassive, dispassionate. They have not yet been stamped with the distortions that mark many of the adults. They lack expressive peculiarities; they do not appear either happy or downcast. They merely witness the world around them, patiently waiting to take over the stage as players.

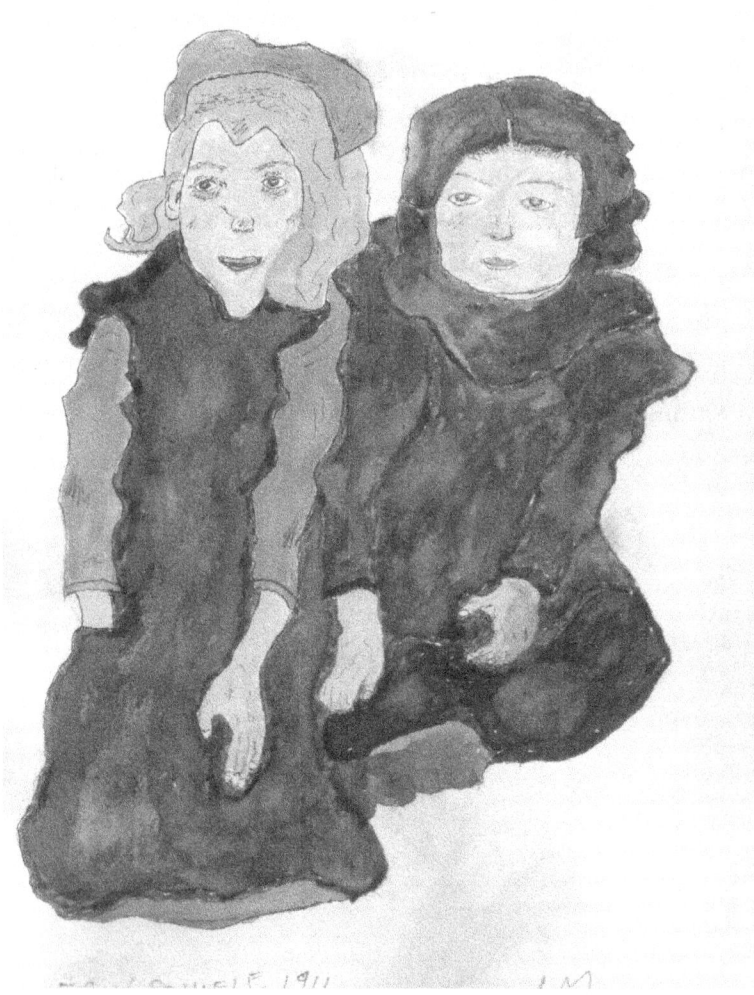

Egon Schiele, 1911

Faces of Children

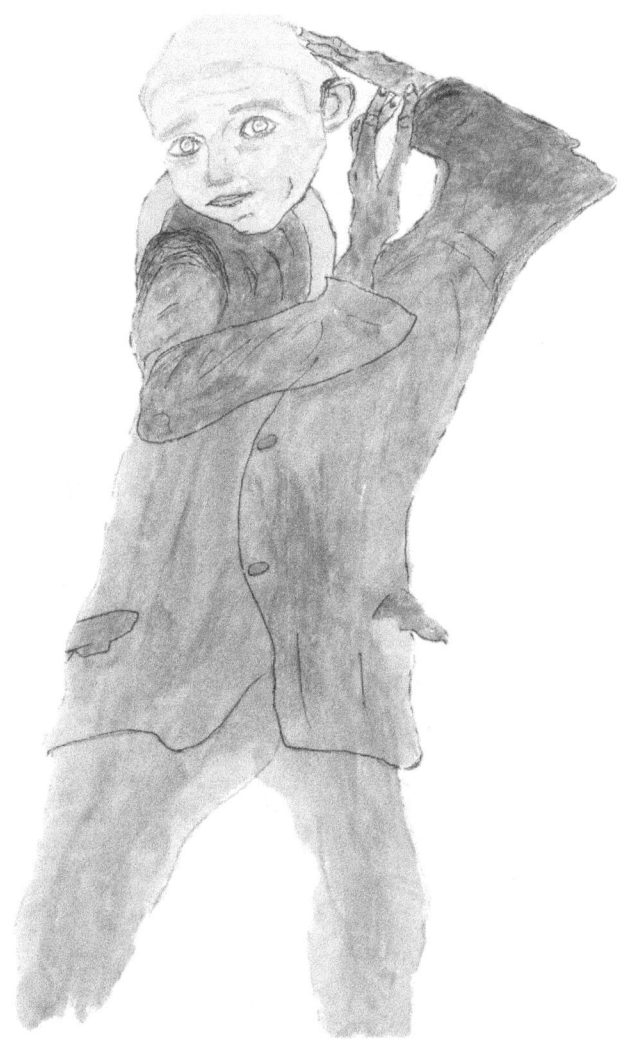

Egon Schiele, 1910

Imagery in Art and Literature

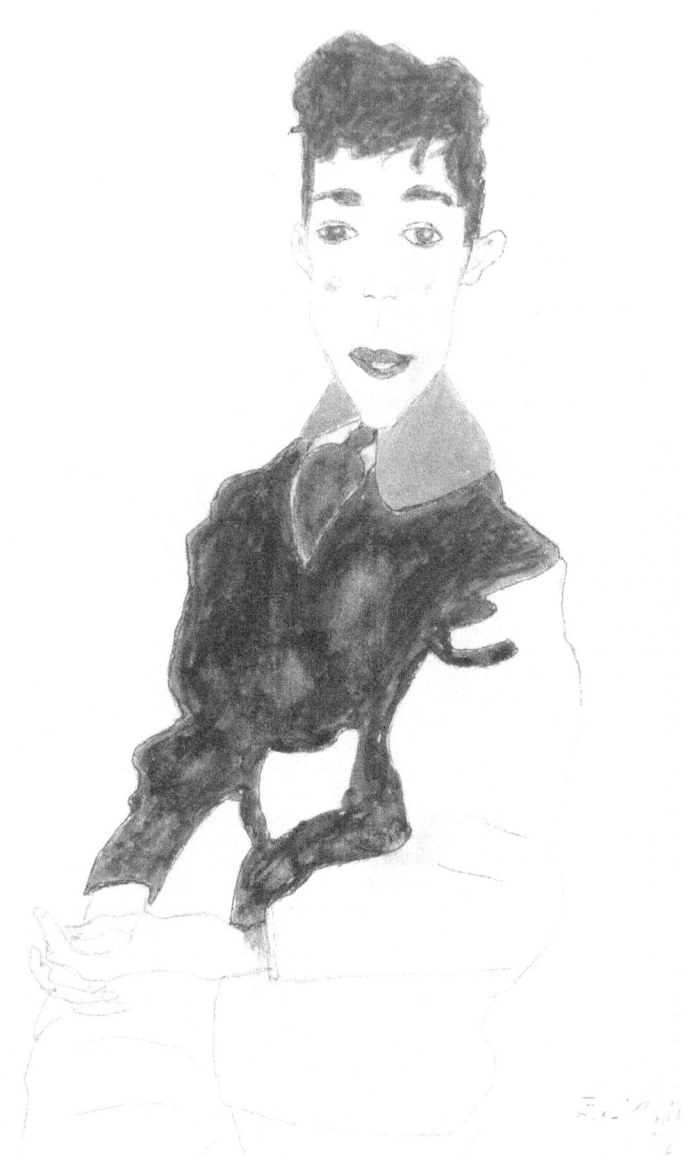

Egon Schiele, 1913

Faces of Children

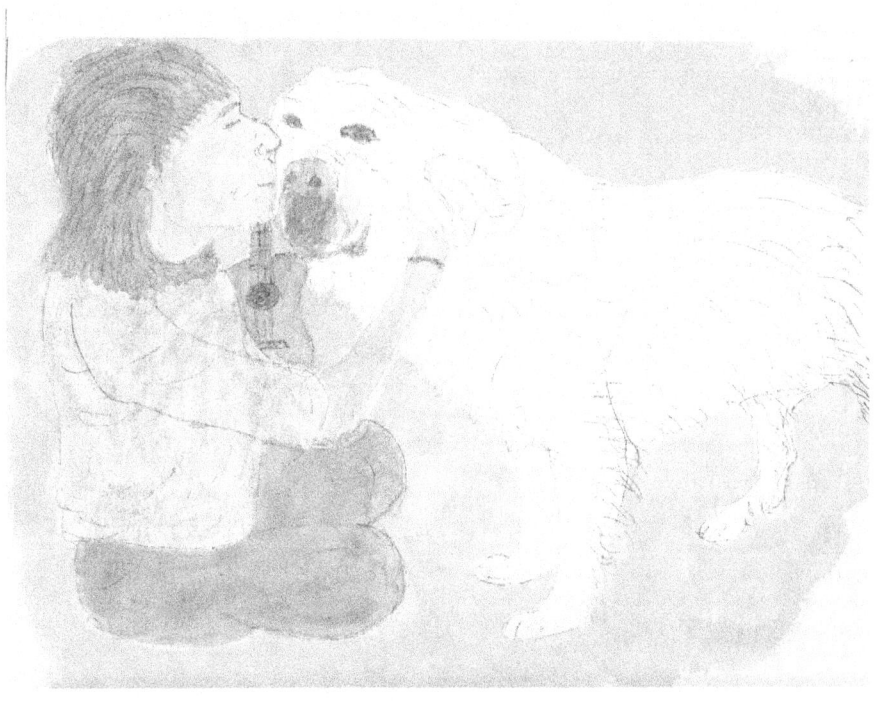

Len Moss, 2017

6
Faces of Age

Physical decline, loss of power or status, and death are ancient subjects explored in tragic literature and art. We travel a long, often difficult road from youth to old age. Artists witness identity changes in facial features and body postures at the final stage of the journey.

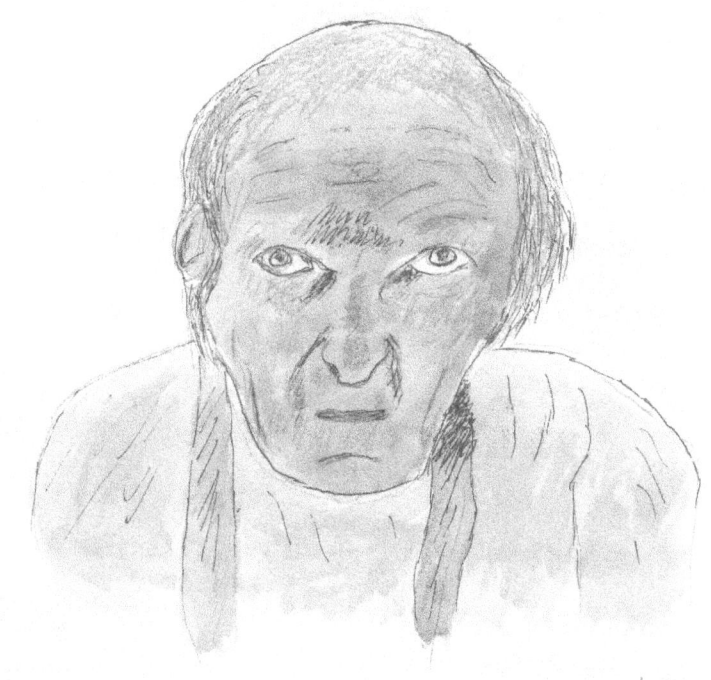

Gustav Klimt, 1895

Imagery in Art and Literature

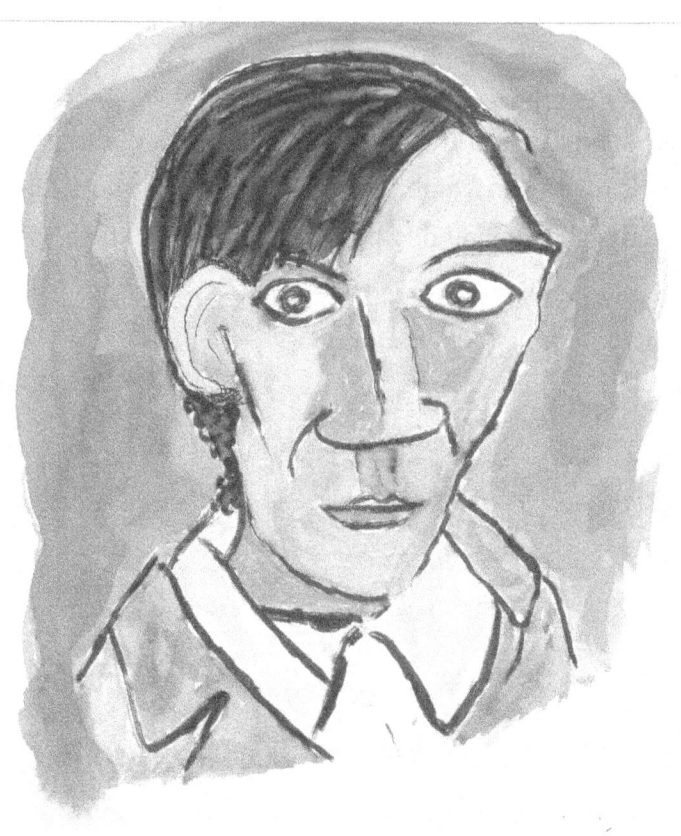

Self-Portrait at Age 25, Pablo Picasso, 1907

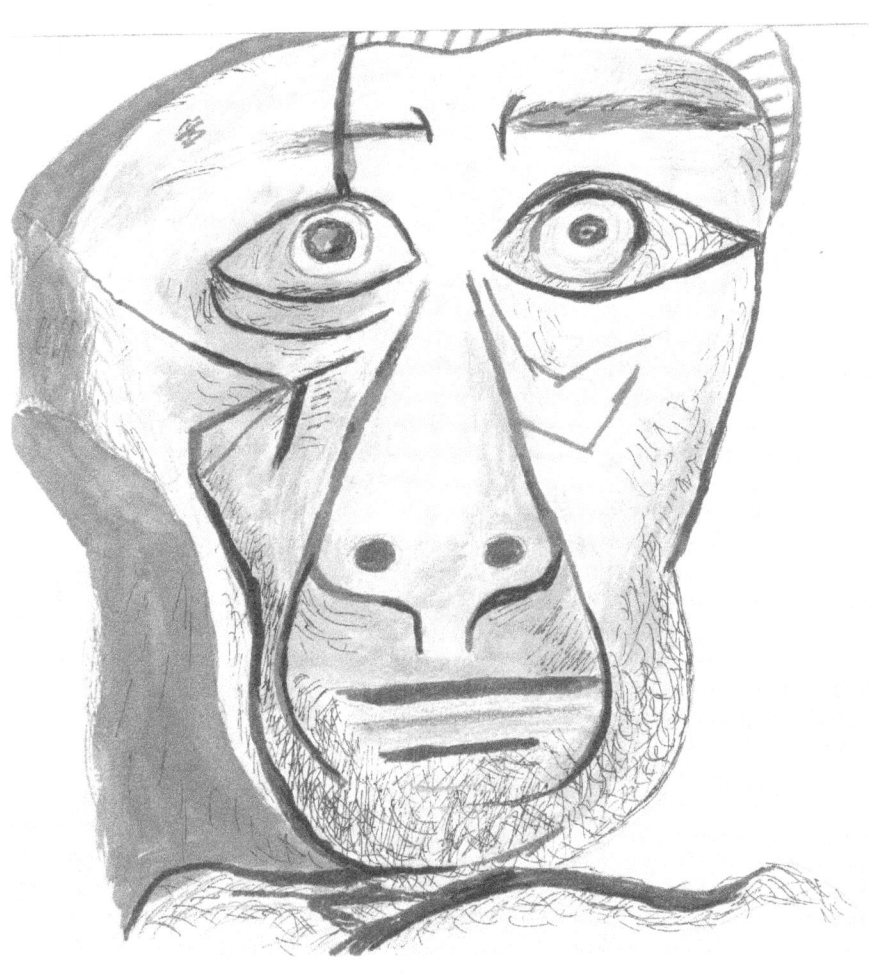

Self-Portrait at Age 90, Pablo Picasso, 1972

Part II

The Image in Literature

7
Simplicity and Irony

Hamlet and The Bible

Literary images commonly reflect competition between contrasting identities linked in contradiction. Jesus in the New Testament recruits simple images to make the argument with his adversaries understandable to his audience of farmers, shepherds, fishermen, merchants, and carpenters. He needed an uncomplicated vehicle to serve as his message carrier, so he drafted familiar, down-to-earth metaphors to supplement his historical parallels, miracles, and other story components.

He calls upon easily recognized verbal pictures, a "secret" language of instruction that his largely illiterate listeners could readily grasp but would remain indecipherable to his detractors. In the manner of Scriptural authors like Isaiah, he draws upon prosaic images and parables that connote crucial meanings in familiar language. They give pictorial immediacy to his struggle with enemies.

Negative images represent his critics—a "blind guide," a viper's brood or nest, homeless unclean spirits, an unforgiving debtor, murderous vineyard tenants, indifferent wedding guests, a rich man without pity for the poor, an early guest who nevertheless finishes the day "last," evil tenants who kill the landowner's son, undeserving wedding guests, a bullying servant, improvident maids, a lazy investor. These veiled allusions imply censure of leaders who cannot redefine their Covenant, like seeds that fall on rocky soil or weeds that will be burned.

Other images present affirmative pictures—a naïve child, the throne or house (the legacy) of David, the "sign of the prophet Jonah," laborers' equal pay, a homeowner and his "trusty servant," a well-cultivated vineyard that reflects its caretaker's prudence. They lend tangible substance to a positive concept. Like the negative metaphors, they each project one meaning with one carrier.

At other times Jesus contrasts *two* images in a pairing of opposites, two physical carriers that invoke contrary meanings—faithful and wayward servants, houses built on rock or sand, seeds sown on rocky and on fertile ground, foolish maids and a bridegroom, energetic or lazy investors. In each pair, one connotation opposes its antithesis.

In using imagery to attack his opponents, Jesus often attaches an explanation, combining metaphor with explanation:

> No servant can be the slave of two masters; for either he will hate the first and love the second, or he will be devoted to the first and think nothing of the second. You cannot serve God and Money. (*Matthew* 6.24)

> Do not give dogs what is holy; do not throw your pearls to the pigs: they will only trample on them, and turn and tear you to pieces . . . .. Beware of false prophets, men who come to you dressed up as sheep while underneath they are savage wolves. (7.6, 7.15)

> Can grapes be picked from briars, or figs from thistles? In the same way, a good tree always yields good fruit, and a poor tree bad fruit. A good tree cannot bear bad fruit, or a poor tree good fruit . . . .. That is

Simplicity and Irony

why I say you will recognize [good and bad prophets] by their fruits. (7.16-20)

Besides its usefulness in criticizing his enemies, expository imagery gives concrete substance to a theoretical program that neither duplicates nor abandons the existing moral code. It identifies a successor to the Hebrew Covenant in tangible terms:

When, therefore, a teacher of the law has become a learner in the kingdom of Heaven, he is like a householder who can produce from his store both the new and the old. (13.52)

Neither do you put new wine into old wineskins; if you do, the skins burst, and then the wine runs out and the skins are spoilt. No, you put new wine into fresh skins; then both are preserved. (9.17)

Jesus delivers an expository metaphor during the traditional Passover celebration, giving a symbolic meaning to the ritual wine. "For this is my blood," he explains, "the blood of the [new] covenant, shed for many for the forgiveness of sins" (26.28). The mystical substitution of self-sacrifice for animal sacrifice advances the evolution from one Covenant to its successor. "How [else] could the scriptures be fulfilled, which say that this must be? . . . This has all happened to fulfill what the prophets wrote" (26.54, 26.56).

When Jesus expands explicated metaphors still further with homespun story lines, bringing together image, explanation, and narrative, he enlists the parable, a venerable literary device previously advanced by Isaiah, among others. It usually comes with an explicit lesson that refashions Scriptural concepts. The combination of homely images, blunt lessons, and familiar folktales addresses common people rather than an educated elite; the most notable example is the parable of the sower (13.1-44).

Matthew credits Isaiah with prior use of this everyday yet "secret" language. Isaiah supposedly said "I will open my mouth in parables; / I will utter things kept secret since the world was made" (Matthew 13.34-35). Matthew is actually quoting Psalms 78.2, but in conceding priority to Isaiah, he has acknowledged his debt to an ancient communication technique in order to reconcile traditional beliefs with current innovations.

It may have been politically as well as pedagogically expedient to speak to ordinary folks in metaphors when attacking Hebrew rivals or revealing heretical "secrets of the kingdom of Heaven." "That is why I speak to them in parables," Jesus says (13.13), paraphrasing Isaiah (6.9-10). The "learned and wise" religious partisans of Jerusalem—Pharisees, high priests, lawyers, Sadducees, and "false prophets"--were accustomed to legalistic exegesis. They had devised an specialized esoteric language to protect their inherited status. But they "look without seeing, and listen without hearing or understanding." Their rituals cannot register the "good news."

On occasion, however, Jesus deciphers his figurative language for his antagonists. Mixing metaphors in the tale about vicious vineyard keepers, he quotes Psalm 118.22-23 to relate his version of Covenantal Law to the solid rock stubbornly spurned by construction supervisors:

> Have you never read in the scriptures: "The stone which the builders rejected has become the main corner-stone. This is the Lord's doing, and it is wonder-

> ful in our eyes"? Therefore, I tell you, the kingdom of
> God will be taken away from you, and given to a nation that yields the proper fruit. (21.42-44)

The unreceptive "builders" (chief priests and Pharisees), enlightened once the speaker explains his symbolic code, belatedly "saw that he was referring to them."

How relevant to real life are the metaphorical constructions reviewed here? How accurate are the simple and complex images that purport to represent actual identities? Do they convey ethical, psychological, or historical truths? Some techniques like the parable make an obvious assumption of authenticity, but is the assumption valid? Is figurative language necessarily fictional?

The carrier of an image is neither true nor false; instead, it is either effective or ineffective as a vehicle designed to carry a concept or quality. The quality or concept may indeed be true or false when viewed as an abstraction, but it is incomplete without the mediation of a concrete carrier. The biblical image is not solely a literary invention *or* a bald statement of truth; it integrates the two in a novel format. It presents a unique *merger* of a verbal medium describing a familiar figure or object and a verbal message entailing an unfamiliar concept. It projects a new, distinctive totality that exerts a strong appeal to the imagination but may not be imaginary.

Sometimes it *is* imaginary. In Hamlet's musings, in contrast to Matthew's account, the designation of competitors remains highly abstract and puzzling; Shakespeare burdened his prince with a philosophical war. The concrete rivalry between good and evil carriers pictured by biblical parables turns into an inconclusive division between theoretical adversaries, an allegorical opposition between angelic and animal identities. The images convey generalized, intangible meanings. Their conflict resists comprehension as well as conciliation.

The imagery opens out from a private quandary to a universal dilemma when Hamlet speculates that all humanity is locked in a battle of "mighty opposites." Man, starting with Adam, may be "in action how like an angel, in apprehension how like a god," but he regresses to the status of "a beast, no more." The unresolved result is that he is both "noble in reason, infinite in faculties" and "rank and gross in nature." He acts "greatly . . . when honour's at the stake" but often behaves like "a rogue and peasant slave," a "dull and muddy-mettled rascal" given over to "bestial oblivion."

This antithesis reflected the widespread view of humanity as a battleground between primitive emotion and civilized intelligence, between "noble" reason and "gross" animality. Depicting human deficiencies with animal images was a popular practice in biblical, classical, and European literature. The "beast" image usually connoted ungoverned impulse or predatory self-interest, biological urges that clashed with rational principles.

But for Hamlet these general categories, unlike readily recognizable biblical terms, remain arbitrary, subject to a variety of interpretations. They verge on the metaphysical. Who has seen an angel? Is it possible to conceive a man or woman wholly as a "beast, no more"? Good and evil expressed by such intangible concepts may be hard to grasp even for highly educated and articulate spokesmen. What might seem simple can turn into a vague abstraction in need of further interpretation.

Voiced in those terms, of course, the pairing serves a definite dramatic purpose. Shakespeare designed it to refer to the hero's confusion and ambivalence. When Hamlet gives equal status to godlike reason and "bestial oblivion," he splits the human personality into nebulous factions, angel and beast. He thereby condemns himself (and mankind) to an insoluble self-contradiction, to ceaseless vacillation between hypothetical adversaries. He becomes irretrievably suspended between intangible categories.

The antithesis is still a common cliché, an arbitrary distinction that precludes any possibility of harmonizing absolute categories. Hamlet's quandary reflects an ill-defined antagonism between "divinity" and instinct that, in the absence of clarification by some transcendent authority, leads to an unsolvable outcome.

Whether familiar or imaginary, the rivalries delineated by the paired metaphors of Jesus and Hamlet, while relevant to argumentative or dramatic purpose, are stationary. Neither the carrier nor its meaning changes: fixed sensory contours reflect fixed concepts, whether easily identifiable or metaphysical. Virtue is virtue, evil is evil; they are unvarying.

In traditional fashion, light represents a constellation of positive values—virtue, renewal, permanence, safety, health, knowledge, order. Darkness, the polar contrast, typically implies uncertain, transitional, or negative states—evil, death, danger and fright, sickness, falsehood or illusion, chaos ("night without end of the abyssal depths," a character remarks in *Waiting for Godot*).

In more complex figurative constructions, however, antithetic meanings become variable and mobile. Light and darkness, commonly paired in a conventional dualism (duel-ism) as inflexible, unchanging adversaries, may be transformed in appearance and reversed in value. Light can successively or simultaneously imply both wholesome energy and decay; darkness may imply both peace and despair. The Book of Job offers a fine example in some detail of this metaphorical versatility. Light and dark *each* transmits contradictory connotations. They each project the advisers' orthodoxy, Job's inconsistency, and a "mystery" that transcends both.

Conventional usage is still evident. God states that Job's "ignorant words / cloud my design in darkness." Eliphaz identifies night with "anxious visions" and "terror" (4.13-14) or with the wrongdoing of "schemers" who replace daylight with night (5.14, 22.11). According to Bildad, "it is the wicked whose light is extinguished" (18.5). Zophar insists that the godless person "will fly away like a dream and be lost, / driven off like a vision of the night" (20.8). And in the view of Elihu, God punishes bad men at night (34.25, 36.21).

Job too, like Samson in Milton's play about another benighted biblical figure, allocates negative meanings to night in order to delineate his predicament. Nighttime dreams sent by God can be terrifying (7.14), darkness may signify death (10.20-22, 14.1-2) or ignorance (12.22-24). God formerly dispelled darkness with guidance and protection (29.1-3), but no more. "I looked for light but there came darkness" (30.26), Job complains. He curses "the day of his birth" in synonymous phrasing:

> May that day turn into darkness; may God above not look for it,
> nor light of dawn shine on it.
> May blackness sully it, and murk and gloom,
> cloud smother that day, swift darkness eclipse its sun.
> Blind darkness swallow up that night. (3.4-6)

For Job, as for the narrator of the Book of Ecclesiastes, night often signifies moral and physical blight or intellectual and emotional turmoil that overwhelms the positive power of light.

The customary connotations of this polarity seem clear enough, unwavering and invariable, but cultural dilemmas, like natural processes, are often complex (ironic). The author of the Book of Job soon supplants the common associations. Constant meanings become reversed: darkness may be constructive, light unreliable. Conversion, reversal of identity, replaces simple opposition. Light has been corrupted and transformed, not merely vanquished, by darkness: "day is turned into night, / and morning light is darkened before me" (17.12). Light no longer retains its traditional meaning but becomes an emissary of darkness.

The significance of that fearful conversion differs according to the observer's perspective. What appears to be destructive or unpredictable to a limited understanding may be fertile and productive from a more comprehensive viewpoint. Darkness may conceal a beneficial "mystery," some unknowable divine purpose. God makes the point explicit. He contends that darkness represents more than evil or the defects of mortality. It is a sign of omniscience:

> Have the gates of death been revealed to you?
> Have you ever seen the doorkeepers of the place of darkness?
> Have you comprehended the vast expanse of the world?
> Come, tell me all this, if you know.
> Which is the way to the home of light
> and where does darkness dwell? . . .
>
> who put wisdom in depths of darkness
> and veiled understanding in secrecy? (38.17-19, 38.36)

Darkness screens the unknowable secrets of the universe; it "hides" divine knowledge. Conventional contraries like life and death, truth and ignorance, virtue and evil cannot restrict that knowledge. Neither the obscure, "mysterious" workings of God nor "the vast expanse of the world" can be symbolized by tidy polarities of light and darkness. And even this exposure to converted darkness does not impel Job to recant:

> It is God who makes me faint-hearted
> and the Almighty who fills me with fear,
> yet I am not reduced to silence by the darkness
> nor by the mystery which hides him. (23.16-17)

Sight and blindness, another paired metaphor common also in Athenian tragedy, develops this paradoxical relationship between truth and uncertainty. Again, literary language speaks with an ironic vocabulary: we see, yet do not see. "The land is given over to the power of the wicked, / and the eyes of its judges are blindfold," Job announces (9.24), but Zophar rejoins that it is Job who is blind (11.20), while Eliphaz mocks Job by quoting him:

> But you say, "What does God know?
> Can he see through thick darkness to judge?
> His eyes cannot pierce the curtain of the clouds
> as he walks to and fro on the vault of heaven." (22.13-14)

God not only "sees through darkness" but may, Elihu claims, send corrective visions to men through dreams (33.15-18), thereby making dreams night-messengers of insight and peace as well as ignorance and unrest—a metaphorical enigma referred to by dramatists from Aeschylus to O'Neill. Ambivalent imagery in the Book of Job reflects incongruity with greater fluidity than the fixed borders of Jesus' parables or Hamlet's angel-beast dualism.

But Matthew too communicates metaphorical ambivalence by reporting the conversion of light and darkness, probably the most serviceable paired metaphors in ancient literature. The two carriers still convey a conventional polar opposition between justice and evil, or truth and ignorance, or constancy and deviation.

> The lamp of the body is the eye. If your eyes are sound, you will have light for your whole body; if the eyes are bad, your whole body will be in darkness. If then the only light you have is darkness, the darkness is doubly dark. (Matthew 6.22-23)

In Matthew's description, however, as in the Book of Job, the images become inverted. Unscrupulous individuals are to blame for the reversal, as Isaiah previously reported:

> Shame on you! You who call evil good and good evil,
> who turn darkness into light and light into darkness. (Isaiah 5.20)

On the Day of Judgment, according to both Jesus and Isaiah, the defeat of evil will be heralded by darkness, not light:

> The stars of heaven in their constellations shall give no light,
> the sun shall be darkened at its rising,
> and the moon refuse to shine. (Isaiah 13.10)
>
> The sun will be darkened, the moon will not give her light, the stars will fall from the sky, the celestial powers will be shaken. (Matthew 24.29)

Ultimately, light shining from God's agents will dispel darkness, correct the inversion, and resume its usual role:

> The people who walked in darkness have seen a great light: light has dawned upon them, dwellers in a land as dark as death. (Isaiah 9.2)
>
> He was transfigured; his face shone like the sun, and his clothes became white as the light. (Matthew 17.2)
>
> You are light for all the world. . . . And you, like the lamp, must shed light among your fellows, so that, when they see the good you do, they may give praise to your Father in heaven. (Matthew 5.14, 5.16)

Matthew and Job testify to the operation of ambiguity in biblical literature; metaphorical complexity mirrors moral perplexity. To connote the conversion of ethical principle as well as rivalry between standpoints, they call upon the most useful and best known pair of images in both biblical chronicle and Athenian drama.

Irony in the Oresteia

A similar conception was imagined in the other literary tradition that shaped Western culture; the three known Athenian playwrights dramatized the theme extensively. Aeschylus, founder of tragic drama, witnessed a paradoxical reversal of gender identities in his trilogy, the *Oresteia,* a scandalous variation of the longstanding quarrel between male and female temperaments. And the reversal is appropriately exposed by light and darkness fluctuations.

Although generally regarded as a stalwart defender of moral propriety, Aeschylus contrived equivocal sequences and "dream" metaphors that transmit the duplexity of sacrosanct models. Inconsistent characters display contradictory positions; widely popular and admired heroic stereotypes tout "constancy" but hurtle back and forth between a commendable persona and its opposite, jumping from noble values to ruinous degradation, and even when relatively consistent or favored by the gods their antisocial actions induce community uncertainty and distress.

They are prone not simply to a *succession* of high principle alternating with ignoble behavior, but to a paradoxical *simultaneity*. They are not *transformed* by a novel identity; they *revert* to an existing negative predisposition. During military or political conflict, they relapse to their inherent barbarity, the status of a "savage." They remain suspended between both ethical antitheses and emotional contraries.

All three Athenian dramatists delivered critiques of the stereotypical masculine persona, whether embodied in a male or a female, showing it to compose inseparable attitudes that were simultaneously laudable and deplorable, producing ironic consequences. The hero was loyal to the community yet at the same time ego-centered; exemplary yet ignoble; strongly motivated yet subject to spiritless relinquishment; resilient, resourceful, and invincible yet obsessive and vulnerable; unyielding and relentless yet mutable and unstable; wise and responsible yet irrational, impulsive, and self-contradictory; civilized and sophisticated yet primitive, crude, and barbaric; clever and clear-minded yet mindless and confused; aggressive yet defensive; articulate yet speechless; unique yet predictable and bound by tradition; pious yet irreverent.

The *Oresteia* trilogy communicates that convergence of opposites in its imagery. In a remarkable exercise of artistic expertise, Aeschylus calls upon contradictory connotations exhibited by both light and darkness to reflect ambiguous consequences. Like male and female antagonists, light and darkness do not merely combat; they exchange their traditional roles. Metaphorical fluctuation indicates moral fluctuation.

The first play of the trilogy inaugurates the irony: an unwavering female controls a mutable male chorus. Clytemnestra, performing like a "manly" model, remains steadfast in intelligence, courage, eloquence, and leadership strategy, repelling every challenge to her authority. The Argive elders, in contrast, express perplexity, fear, and disorientation despite their sporadic attempts to assert masculine status. They cautiously question their ruler's actions but defer to them. Their hesitation and inconstancy are overshadowed by the aggressiveness of the Queen, even though like many aristocratic males she debases the standards she claims to uphold after taking a lover and assassinating by her husband.

Clytemnestra's inconsistency is reproduced by the variability of light. Light takes on the properties of darkness, and darkness shows the same convertibility. Fluid metaphors emulate the confusing inversions of stereotypical roles. To prepare for these unconventional inversions, Aeschylus first installs the customary association of light with reliability, health, and optimism. *Agamemnon* opens in a cheerful mood. Before dawn, a beacon fire signals the fall of Troy, an event promising deliverance to different individuals for different reasons—to Agamemnon, who had found it necessary to sacrifice his daughter to achieve victory; to Clytemnestra, bereaved by the loss of her daughter and deprived of her husband during the war; to the Argive townsfolk, troubled by matters known or not yet disclosed; and to the watchman, after his tedious vigil.

"Now let there be again redemption from distress," the watchman prays, "the flare burning from the blackness in good augury." Disturbed by a danger he dares not name, he hopes that the "blaze of the darkness" will dispel the miseries of night, that a "harbinger of day's / shining" will be an auspicious "prelude" to great joy. The distant flickering of the beacon anticipates the stronger light of dawn; in the same way, his hope may soon be magnified.

Clytemnestra's thirty-five-line review of the beacon's progress develops this theme more fully. The queen's signal fires overcame the distance from Troy to Argos just as the fire of the Achaeans overcame the Trojan nation: one victory epitomized the other. When Clytemnestra imagines the flaming beacon as a "flare in exultation" leaping across Aegean islands to telegraph the most glorious triumph of the age, the vivid details of her description come across as *her* triumph.

Her terminology extracts a climactic, almost sexual vision from the "bright message." "Timbers flaming into gold" were "like the sunrise." The "far–thrown" blazes grew "stronger" as they advanced, building a "stintless heaping force." She proclaims the transition from night to bright day as prelude to a corresponding renaissance in the kingdom. Then sacrificial flames replace the beacons in the brilliance of day, completing her prediction of peace and happiness by invoking divine favor.

The herald articulates this idea of beneficent light emerging from darkness and signaling victory. His narration of the army's disastrous return voyage recounts the dangers encountered during a terrible night storm at sea. The only light that fell upon the destruction and chaos was given off by burning ships. Yet relief came with the dawn of a "pale sky;" the "sun's gleam," though feeble, meant survival. The herald gives thanks for his safe arrival "in daylight," hails the "sunlight" of Argos, addresses "divinities that face the sun," and announces the imminent return of Agamemnon "bearing light in the gloom."

All these reassuring signs of the resumption of light, of course, actually presage the onset of darkness. The Greek audience would know that the "stintless heaping force" of flames and their "bright message" actually foreshadowed (so to speak) an unhappy time for the kingdom. Alerted by the beacon, the queen (with Aegisthus) slaughters Agamemnon and usurps his throne, instituting a dark oppressive regime lasting until Orestes and Electra avenge the murder years later. By the end of *Agamemnon*, the chorus has turned from bright expectations to thoughts of "our sunset . . . as in the hour of death."

The chorus, in fact, voices from the beginning a subdued fearfulness that deflates to some extent the buoyant emotions animating their salutation to light. Choric types insist on conservative guidelines but are intimidated or seduced by a contrary position. While delighted by "sweet hope shining from the [sacrificial] fires," the city elders, aware that Clytemnestra has embarked on a scandalous course, and aware also that several gruesome crimes had already been committed by family members in the past, adopt the skeptical, inconclusive attitude hinted at by the watchman ("the house . . . might speak / aloud and plain"). Dismayed by "perplexity / that grows now into darkness of thought," but not in a position to confess their trepidation openly, they confine their uneasiness to the "darkness of my heart."

They have learned to acquire certainty through experience and hard–headed logic, a guideline that moves them to doubt Clytemnestra's words reporting the Greek victory in Troy. Night carries dubious information, "dreams of dark fancy," but sunrise illuminates facts, not visions. "All will come clear in the next dawn's sunlight." Darkness portends deceit, illusion, and ignorance, in addition to horrendous negatives like destruction, fear, and evil.

They respond to Clytemnestra's victory proclamation, therefore, by wondering whether a mere dream produced it in the night. For the chorus, dreams are unreliable messengers; they can be double–dealing, half light and half shadow, like beacon fires and burning ships. One may act without wisdom by crediting "a dream that falters in the daylight." The queen rebuts the accusation, but the elders repeat their misgivings. The "beacon's bright message," the "interchange of flame and flame . . . may be real" or it may be illusory. "Bright and dreamwise ecstasy / in light's appearance might have charmed our hearts awry." Light can represent hope and at the same time presage disaster.

Along the same lines, Menelaus fancies his absent wife "shining in dreams" though "it is vain to dream and to see splendours." Only the clairvoyant Cassandra respects the dream state, describing the murdered children of Thyestes "imaged as in the shadow of dreams." But since no one can fathom her enigmatic visions, she yearns for the day when her information will be comprehensible, "bright and strong / as winds blow into morning and the sun's uprise." In the meantime, the chorus members, puzzled by her suspension between truth and nonsense, remain in "darkness." "We want no prophets," they reply. Her words are merely obscure to them, not ambiguous. While they do not take dreams seriously, they can hardly distinguish fantasy or falsehood from reality.

Agamemnon's return in daylight does not dispel their lack of clarity. Foreboding and "dreams of dark fancy" persistently spoil their "good hope":

> I murmur deep in darkness
> sore at heart; my hope is gone now
> ever again to unwind some crucial good
> from the flames about my heart.

Here, as before in the herald's storm description, flames reveal a dark side of abnormality and distress that dominates their association with uplifted spirits. At the same time that Clytemnestra, the herald, and the watchman look to fire as the harbinger of new life, Cassandra and the chorus predict the arrival of peril, depression, and guilt with images that participate in both camps.

Just as the chorus wavers between affirmation and rejection, light is never free of shadow. By the same token, darkness is not without constructive potential; it may configure essential values. When the city's elders condemn evil, they conceive justice in terms of darkness as well as light. Since they dare not name the current evildoers, they must restrict their comments either to previous crimes involving Thyestes, Atreus, and Paris, or to the workings of morality in general. In those general terms they picture a network in which good and evil events share or exchange traditional properties. He who spurns virtue, they meditate, "burns to evil beauty," to flaming darkness where retribution waits "in the hooded night." "The black Furies," agents of justice, hunt the criminal and "drop him to darkness." "Men's dark actions," incited by pride, are punished by "black visaged Disasters" or by a "dark angel."

Thus the sinner and her crimes, but also her judges and punishment, are all black. At the same time, "righteousness," veiled by deep shade, glows as "a shining in / the smoke of mean houses." Good and evil do not lose their primary natures, but they interact endlessly and sometimes become almost indistinguishable. Multifaceted light—salvation, peace, justified revenge, truth—disputes with but also comports with darkness—death, suffering, sin, illusion.

Life and happiness may bring death and grief; what one calls righteousness another calls vice. Light and darkness do not merely challenge each other in perpetual combat; they each participate in the other, with flames, dreams, and prophecies serving as their intermediaries. They are mercurial, like the tragic hero whose commitment to noble behavior carries the potential for *irrational* behavior, two sides of one coin.

In the second and third plays of the trilogy, Aeschylus resumes his ingenious orchestration of light and dark (along with blood imagery) in order to resolve the issue raised by his bold heroine. Though immune to change as she confidently validates the assassination, Clytemnestra has exposed her pernicious side and prompted insecurity in others. Her scandalous deed has thrown Argos into a state of anxiety that ends with her death, the defeat of her claim to righteousness, and the resumption of male dominance.

The Libation Bearers arouses the customary expectation raised at the start of *Agamemnon*: light may finally supersede the darkness of cruelty, cynicism, shame. This time, however, Clytemnestra is less confident as she prays for deliverance from darkness. Haunted by memories of the killing and "shaken in the night," she lights torches to relieve the "blind dark" of her fear. Female servants lament the terror that arises as "a cry in night's suffering." They bemoan the "sunless" ruin of their once–great court, and ask divine powers to release the injured parties from their "helm of darkness."

And again, polar images engage in weird intimacy. The servants dress in black to demonstrate their loyalty to Electra. They despise evil whether it strikes in "brightness" or "in gloom of half dark" or in "desperate night." Orestes has vowed to eliminate "madness and empty terror in the night"; he plans to placate his father's shade with "light that will match your dark," yet he invokes "the dark arrow of the dead men underground."

His vengeance will unavoidably be punished by black Furies, but it will "kindle a flame / and light of liberty," enabling him and his sister to "look on the shining of daylight" when "light [will be] here to behold." The chorus seconds his goal: although matricide may be a "dark" deed, it will be a "light" to "fall on the man [Aegisthus] who killed."

In the third play, *The Eumenides*, revenge does indeed plunge Orestes into the shadow that had benighted his mother's "dark heart." Although he acted in accordance with the "luminous evidence of Zeus," the Furies, "daughters of the night," insist that a matricide cannot escape his sin:

He falls, and does not know in the daze of his folly.
Such in the dark of man is the mist of infection
that hovers, and moaning rumor tells how his house lies
under fog that glooms above.

Simplicity and Irony

The Furies possess the double valence possessed by flames and dreams: they are underworld immortals personifying stark terror but also enforcers of primeval law. They draw Orestes, who has discharged a valid obligation to his father, toward their horrors of guilt and death. The actions of *both* sides are at once just and damnable. Positive and negative have again become interchangeable as well as competitive.

But irresolution would be inappropriate for the conclusion. So, having scripted an agitated dialogue between contraries, the dramatist imposes an orderly conciliation. To settle the moral–metaphorical issue and release his actors from the profound muddle at the intersection of light and dark, Aeschylus commemorates the mythical metamorphosis of the Furies. Their darkly repellent retribution for kin murder is to be reformed and relocated in a different jurisdiction.

Under their "gracious" guidance, society will be endowed with good luck, prosperity, and peace. The Furies are going to "put to sleep the bitter strength in the black wave" in renovated underground quarters, where they may "sit on shining chairs" and act as sources of creativity that will "wash over the country in full sunlight." Torches brighten the last scene with "sacred light" during a groundbreaking treaty between "the primeval dark of earth-hollows" and "the sun's bright magnificence." The verdict declared by Athena at the trial of Orestes predicts rapport, neither conflict nor flux, between messengers of light and newly converted, benevolent agents of darkness. Orestes stands acquitted of tragic ambiguity.

Are these descriptions sufficient to realize the promised conciliation? Can the daughters of night be so readily enlightened? The playwright's prophetic vision may be just a dream. Despite the patriotic enthusiasm to commemorate an ethical innovation that would enhance the glory and prosperity of Athens, the commemoration falls short of a definitive solution to the deadlock. Orestes' revenge and acquittal do not prove to be entirely commendable when a prejudiced goddess (Athena) nullifies a heroic woman's questionable and dangerous but extraordinary vanity.

The torchlight procession reportedly held in the theater at the conclusion of the trilogy must have been exciting and gratifying for the Athenian spectators, but to a distant reader in our own age the domestication of wildly dark goddesses intent on avenging the murder of a mother seems less convincing. Athena's few remarks about "flaring torches," "sacred light," and "shining chairs" lack enough immediacy and complexity, enough full–bodied metaphorical weight, to indicate a modification of the Furies' basic function as rulers of "the evil darkness of the Pit below." The subordination of darkness to light, and female to male, remains questionable but intact.

Aeschylus did not visualize a fundamental alternative to the ancient role of masculine domination or an alteration that would resolve the ironic exchange of gender roles. Are those roles fixed or fluid or both? He did not eliminate the ambiguity, but he presented it clearly and skillfully to uncover the dilemma raised by heroic enterprise. His images enshrouding light in darkness and darkness in light gave a local habitation and a name to the puzzling interplay between the assertion and relinquishment of noble identity, between constancy and deviation. The brilliance of the *Oresteia* shines in the multifaceted metaphorical and narrative rendering of an unsolved paradox.

Seneca's Simplicity and the Eclipse of Light

Not all classical masters of drama possessed the talent or inclination to play so intriguingly with contrary connotations attached to a commonplace metaphor. Five hundred years after the *Oresteia* was staged, Seneca, the first–century Roman philosopher, statesman, and adapter of Athenian tragedy, took a more restricted view. He did not call upon light and darkness imagery to symbolize a paradoxical subject because the two-sided masculine stereotype revealed by Aeschylus to be simultaneously admirable and deadly had become, for him, obsolete. Even the specious justifications that had been proposed by self-seeking characters in the plays of Aeschylus, Euripides and Sophocles disappear. Seneca's plays deal with unrelieved darkness.

Viewed in the perspective dramatized by the Athenian playwrights, admirable behavior does not require transformation into or adoption of a different, unwholesome personality. It simply alternates with a pre-existing potential. It marks a reversion to the inherent negative side of the dualistic outlook engendered by a "heroic" type. For Seneca, on the other hand, the masculine stereotype is not dualistic; it is not only obsolete but wholly negative. His cynicism was immutable, his dream–pictures consistently hellish.

We shall not belabor the Latin author for this one–sided approach; his control of metaphor was impressive within its limits. But he would have been the first to credit the complexity of his Greek sources, and we can enlarge our understanding of how imagery operates by reviewing the monochromatic strategy in his version of the Oedipus story in the perspective of the intricate allusions to light and darkness we have observed in the *Oresteia*.

Seneca centered his adaptation of the Sophoclean original on the traditional implications of darkness—sickness, insecurity, ignorance, death, and the chief association, evil. A tight, straightforward connection between image and import contributes to an atmosphere of visual and moral obscurity. Night equals blight, the corruption of body and soul. Oedipus spells out the connection: "fog, dense, and black, / Broods over all the land . . .. The murk of hell / Has swallowed up the heavenly citadels." The chorus of Theban elders, though unclear about the cause, agrees on the consequence. The darkness engulfing their kingdom originated in Hades as punishment for some unknown sin. "Black Death has opened his ravenous mouth to devour us."

Allusions to light are not so conventional. Light normally counters darkness with good health and emotional balance, honesty and justice, but Seneca has cleverly rescinded those affiliations. Now light mirrors neither hope nor false hope, as it does in *Agamemnon*. The life–nourishing sun has been so severely infected by evil that it has lost its ordinary associations and now rises in the murky dawn as an ambassador of the dark, a pessimistic metamorphosis!

Casting a "dull glow," Oedipus explains, the sun "is a torch / Of evil omen," illuminating with its "pale fire" the "havoc of night." Night, lacking stars to alleviate its blackness, had been absolute; now the day, "overcast with clouds," adds to the gloom. Light was not banished; it was corrupted, seduced by its contrary and deprived of its usual merits. Like darkness, it now exerts only one influence, one that goes against our expectations. If Aeschylus juggles positive and negative connotations before eventually rehabilitating light, Seneca's conversion of light remains adamant.

Blind Tiresias expands the subject of darkness triumphant. This character, in legend and Athenian drama, commonly links light with knowledge, darkness with ignorance; though sightless, he can see what is hidden from others. But here again there is a departure from common usage. Enveloped by spiritual darkness, the prophet can glimpse no avenue to redemption. Ordered to interpret the Delphic Oracle's diagnosis of the community's malady, he has no luck searching for information on how to get the "day once more [to] ride brightly in the sky." His sacrificial bull "seemed to fear the daylight, / And shied at the sun's rays."

Beneficial light being in short supply, the sacred flame he kindles quickly goes out. After "dying into blackness," it flares up to give off "dense clouds of smoke enveloping the King, . . . the light of day / Lost in black fog." It is darkness, not light, that reveals information: fog suggests the origin of evil (the unpunished killer of King Laius) as well as the result (Hell's persecution). Seneca replaces light's usual job as emissary of truth with light's new job as infamous participant in perversion and blight, an idea that only halfway repeats Aeschylus' complex practice on the submergence and re-emergence of values.

With blackness reigning over living and dead alike, and light employed as its agent, Tiresias, trying to overcome his deficiencies as a seer, decides to visit Hades, the heart of darkness, there to ask the ghost of Laius to name the murderer. The prophet begins his metaphorical quest, his second search for truth, in a grove outside the city that "was dark as night" even before sunset. When he sets fire to several black oxen and black sheep, his passports to the underworld, a "black void opens" upon sordid "things / Created and concealed in the dark womb / Of everlasting night." From these shadows, the appropriate setting for revelation, he emerges with the answer, designating Oedipus as the disseminator of blackness that properly belongs in Hell.

Seneca completes light's regression with a final twist. He is unwilling to restore light even after the evil afflicting Thebes has been located and Oedipus has paid his debt. Having seen the same dark fact that blind old Tiresias saw, the king puts out his eyes, the better to perpetuate the darkness of that sight:

> He tests his vision, holding up his head
> Against the light, scanning the breadth of sky
> With eyeless holes, to see if all is dark,
> Then tears away the last remaining shreds
> Left of the raggedly uprooted eyes.
> His victory was won; he cried aloud
> To all the gods: "Now spare my country, gods!
> Now justice has been done; my debt is paid.
> Here is the darkness that should fitly fall
> Upon my marriage–bed."

Though he concedes that "there will be brighter skies when I am gone," Oedipus takes on the "blackness that enshrouds my head" as a permanent memorial to his guilt. Since "daylight itself has run away" from him, he will forever comport with "all grim spectres of Disease, black Plague, / Corruption and intolerable Pain!" He will stumble along a "dark road" in exile, "feeling [his way] through the night."

After revelation and retribution, the play ends as gloomily as it began; Oedipus begins and ends in darkness, his subversion as leader and sage heralded by the subversion of light. Metaphor unwaveringly promotes a conspiracy between nightmarish darkness and degraded light; it never reveals contradictory connotations simultaneously residing in the same location, as in the *Oresteia*.

Seneca makes no attempt to copy the virtuosity of Aeschylus, Euripides, and Sophocles by showing self-invalidation as the negative side of noble assertion. Nor does he show a war between antithetic but equally valid positions. He envisioned neither an ironic ebb and flow of resurgent images nor a rivalry enacted by equally self-righteous antagonists. His drama, probably intended for readers rather than the stage, broadcasts a pessimistic conclusion similar to that lamented by Ecclesiastes: traditional virtues have permanently changed for the worse. The Roman playwright and philosopher cannot be accused of cultivating ambiguity.

It is a wonder and a pleasure to see how skillful authors coordinate metaphor with thesis. The argument between Jesus and his critics is represented by the virtuous and evil contestants pictured in down-to-earth parables. Hamlet's irrevocable suspension between abstract contraries gains figurative substance from the impasse between angel and beast. And Seneca is consistent in referring to the power and triumph of darkness. At a more complex level, the Bible and the *Oresteia* entertain metaphorical inversion. Job's negative attitude and final affirmation are each configured by the same images, and Matthew's comments often reflect a similar duality. The language of imagery has many contrivances and many uses.

Nietzsche Explains Ambiguity

Friedrich Nietzsche enunciated his view of ambiguity long after the Biblical chronicles and Athenian drama. Fifty years after Hegel attested to the durability of social laws, he proclaimed their instability. His remarks in *The Birth of Tragedy* (published in 1872) and *The Will to Power* (written 1883–1888, published 1901), among other works, announced the triumph of transience, the impermanence of ethical directives, their absurdity, fluidity, "contingency," and degeneration.

The hero (or antihero) in tragic literature, deprived of noble expectations, sacred coalitions, and "absolute" codes, could no longer claim to be a moral exemplar but rather a witness of the interplay between affirmation and cynicism. His emotional variability deranged his celebrated moral constancy.

Nietzsche proposed the cyclic metamorphosis of values, their assertion, annulment, and rebirth. He saw tragic drama as a vehicle that travels between substance and illusion, between the declaration and negation of identity. He became the prophet of paradox. He celebrated as an "eternal" principle the natural flux of raw energy, "eternal becoming," which he opposed to philosophical or religious abstractions positing "eternal being" or permanent order.

In *The Will to Power* he defined primal power as "sensuality, intoxication, superabundant animality" that dissipates civilized principles and deprives genteel ventures of point and consistency. Unruly "passion," the ugly beast that Hegel had tamed to carry out venerable ethical systems, tramples such pompous pretensions. The frightening impulses that confuse, depress, or intimidate the timid mind (Nietzsche called it the herd mentality) enliven the tragic super–man, nature's aristocrat. They liberate him from preoccupation with hallowed traditions as well as petty personal concerns. Released from confining cultural programs, exceptional individuals glory in the exhilarating rush of "overflowing vitality," in contrast to insecure choric types for whom (to repeat the remark of Heracles in Euripides' *Alcestis*) "life is not really life but a catastrophe."

"The terrors and horrors of existence" could induce fear or resignation to injustice and loss; on the other hand, acquaintance with "terrifying and questionable" insecurities can stimulate an ecstatic "joy," a feeling of "complete oneness with the essence of the universe." Resilient, self–conscious visionaries (male visionaries, in Nietzsche's view) experience ecstasy by embracing a life–renewing, life–rending force:

> For a brief moment we become the primal Being, and we experience its insatiable hunger for existence. Now we

see the struggle, the pain, the destruction of appearances, as necessary, because of the constant proliferation of forms pushing into life, because of the extravagant fecundity of the world will. . . . Pity and terror notwithstanding, we realize our great good fortune in having life—not as individuals, but as part of the life force with whose procreative lust we have become one (*Birth of Tragedy*).

Nietzsche credited his discovery to Heraclitus, his "predecessor" in the sixth century BCE; German thinkers in the nineteenth century never strayed far from Greek poets and philosophers.

The yea–saying to the impermanence and annihilation of things, which is the decisive feature of a Dionysian philosophy; the yea–saying to contradiction and war, the postulation of Becoming, together with the radical rejection even of the concept Being—in all these things, at all events, I must recognize him who has come nearest to me in thought hitherto (*Ecce Homo*).

The eternal and exclusive Becoming, the total instability of all reality and actuality, which continually works and becomes and never *is*, as Heraclitus teaches—is an awful and appalling conception (*Early Greek Philosophy*).

In so far as the senses show us a state of Becoming, of transiency, and of change, they do not lie. In declaring that Being was an empty illusion, Heraclitus will remain eternally right (*Twilight of the Idols*).

Nietzsche derived from Heraclitus a message that human activity revolves in endless succession between flux and repetition, deterioration and restoration. The dissolution or discontinuity or mutation of apparent ethical substances perpetually alternates with reinstatement.

> The doctrine of the "Eternal Recurrence"—that is to say, of the absolute and eternal repetition of all things in periodical cycles—this doctrine of Zarathustra's might, it is true, have been taught [by Heraclitus] (*Ecce Homo*).

The flow of natural energy is not chaotic: in a weird recurring cycle (not a simultaneity), mutation reverses the kaleidoscopic "appearances" of stable identities, social structures, and formal rules, then returns the deranged semblances back to their original condition and the illusion of constancy, reiterating an infinite number of times the shifting façades.

> Everything becomes and recurs eternally—escape is impossible! . . . The law of the conservation of energy demands eternal recurrence: . . . the world as a circular movement that has already repeated itself infinitely often and plays its game in infinitum (*Will to Power*).

Nietzsche viewed tragic art from this Heraclitian perspective. In tragic drama, eternal reiteration complements eternal oscillation. The poet conceives dream–pictures and stories ("mere phantoms") that create an "illusion" of artistic order to mediate the terror and shock of cosmic energy. Playwrights translate an "orgiastic" sense of "vitality and strength" into tales and images that inspire painful exaltation with serene detachment (*Twilight of the Idols*). In the hands of Aeschylus or Sophocles (Euripides gets rejected as a rationalist by Nietzsche and as an irrationalist by Hegel), tragedy becomes "an Apollonian embodiment of Dionysian insights and powers" (*Birth of Tragedy*). Incongruous yet repetitive metaphors transmit at a safe distance the terrible, exhilarating progression of disintegration and reintegration.

Witnessing in a dramatic work this oscillation between discontinuity ("dissonance") and iteration ("recurrence") can lead the spectator either to insanity or enlightenment. Tragic art may instill a sense of futility or else stimulate unruly creativity. Literary products are terribly upsetting when they reveal the disruptive face of reality, but they can instigate "the redemption of the sufferer—the way to states in which suffering is willed, transfigured, deified, where suffering is a form of great delight" (*Will to Power*).

Tragic images thus picture a riotous circular process, at once degenerative and regenerative, rather than a single, well–defined static "truth." "What therefore is truth?" Nietzsche asks in *Early Greek Philosophy* : "a mobile army of metaphors, metonymies, anthropomorphisms.... Truths are illusions,... worn–out metaphors." Even the terms "Apollonian" and "Dionysian" are metaphors that only hint at a rapturous, terrifying vision that supersedes intellectual distinctions, a vision of repeated identities and transformations not attributable to rational causation.

The fluctuating "life force" becomes visible in evanescent pictures that mock permanence, in contrast to a clearly articulated sequence of collisions between noble causes that, according to Hegel, manifests unvarying spiritual order. Nietzsche proposed a dualism that has fascinated the Western mentality for millennia, a fluctuation between positive identity and its negation, authoritarian order and anarchy. Infinite variability replaces infinite constancy.

For Nietzsche all variables and all constancies reflect a single "eternal" power. Tragic drama, he claimed, offers evidence, no matter how illusory, indirect, or problematic, of a controlling force. The dissonant flow of appearances reveals a cosmic presence, a disruptive but creative "begetter of all things" that reconciles integrity with mutation (*Birth of Tragedy*).

This speculation about ultimate causes (Hamlet calls it "a divinity that shapes our ends"), however, does not actually inform most classical and Shakespearean tragedies. The plays focus on tangible contradictions traced in ironic patterns of speech, narrative, and image, not on mystical conjectures about primal essence or energy. Literary procedures rather than philosophical abstractions adequately account for the convergence of moral plenitude and deprivation, loss and restitution, without a need for transcendent supervision. But apart from a claim to superior power, Nietzsche's theory on inevitable self-contradiction can be considered entirely relevant to the fluctuation experienced by tragic figures.

Two Twentieth-Century Plays

Does light energize or intrude? Is darkness comforting or maddening? The answer to these questions is "both." This metaphorical paradox has represented moral perplexity in Western drama, chronicles, and philosophy from ancient time to the present. Aeschylus visualized their bilateral functioning in his critique of the heroic model; Biblical texts commented on their mysterious duplexity; and Nietzsche, following Heraclitus, described their ambivalence at a philosophical level.

Simplicity and Irony

Among many plays that repeat the irony, two twentieth-century works can be cited--Eugene O'Neill's *Long Day's Journey into Night* (completed in 1941 but not published until 1956, after the author's death) and Samuel Beckett's *Waiting for Godot* (first performed in French in 1953, then published in English a year later).

The characters in *Long Day's Journey into Night* frequently express ethical complexity, but since they are not stabilized by the intervention of man or God they end in an unresolved, everlasting suspension of contraries—an endless fluctuation between stable and converted identities reflected by ambiguous imagery. Light and darkness are each two-faced, double-dealing in moral import. Each retains its association with traditional values yet at same time becomes identified with its antithesis, lapsing into a contrary connotation—an absurdity that frustrates and disrupts its victims. The title connotes a sad journey to uncertainty.

The absurdity is not without a certain logic. Because the vitality, optimism, affection, and clarity usually associated with daylight are severely stressed, an intermission at night is actually a blessing, a release. A journey into darkness may be lamentable, and yet it delivers characters from their repetitive rounds of delusion, criticism, and evasion. Light displays a similar ambiguity, carrying both positive and negative consequences. Light and darkness are equivalent in efficacy as well as toxicity.

The paired images at first seem unidimensional, not equivocal. If light is good, darkness is bad, the symbol of emotional and moral negation. An unpleasant gloom inhabits and surrounds the house:

> *It is around midnight. The lamp in the front hall has been turned out, so that now no light shines through the front parlor. In the living room only the reading lamp on the table is lighted. Outside the windows the*

wall of fog appears denser than ever. (stage directions)

Mary Tyrone identifies this dimness with her husband's miserliness. "Why don't you light the light, James?" she asks; "there's no sense letting your fear of the poorhouse make you too stingy." After Edmund turns on the hall lamp, Tyrone tries, "a bit drunkenly," to resist a miserly impulse to darken the house, but finally gives up, turning off all the "extra lights." His thrift, together with the effect of "booze," Jamie comments, will "put the lights out" in man and house. Darkness connotes an unhealthy, sometimes comic disorientation (drunken Jamie trips on the dark front steps).

But darkness can also connote solace. It may mercifully hide abrasive truths, in contrast to the brutal "glare" of bright light when "all five bulbs of the chandelier in the front parlor are turned on" revealing Mary's pathetic regression to an innocent convent girl (Mad Ophelia). Light shows truth, but too much insight might be as paralyzing as not enough. Darkness, in contrast, aided by morphine or alcohol, conceals truth, and that can be a release from pain.

O'Neill complements this reversal of traditional associations with fog imagery. Initially, fog only deepens the obscurity: Mary urges the men to "take advantage of the sunshine before the fog comes back." Although daytime should bring "fresh air and sunshine," after noon "no sunlight comes into the room." Their discomfort gradually develops into dread as the scene grows hazier ("there's gloom in the air you could cut with a knife"). "We're in for another night of fog, I'm afraid," Tyrone announces, and the family's turmoil increases as the fog descends and a "damned" foghorn, "moaning like a mournful whale in labor," signals the transition to darkness.

Fog, however, like night, is double-dealing. At the same time that it deepens her isolation ("why is it fog makes everything sound so sad and lost?"), it permits Mary to return to memories of blissful youth—her journey into the release facilitated by night. "I really love fog," she says. "It hides you from the world and the world from you. You feel that everything has changed, and nothing is what it seemed to be. No one can find or touch you any more."

The "melancholy moan of the foghorn" benevolently recalls her lost faith ("it keeps reminding you, and warning you, and calling you back"), and the darkness delivers her from evil ("it will soon be night, thank goodness"). Fog may be "dismal" ("it's very dreary and sad to be here alone in the fog with night falling"), but the darkness allows Mary to withdraw to a drug-induced hallucination of religious tranquility, the conclusion she had sought and lost in daylight. Edmund makes the point explicit: "the hardest thing to take is the blank wall she builds around her. Or it's more like a bank of fog in which she hides and loses herself."

Yet Edmund considers himself one of the "fog people" too. He feels "alone, lost in the fog"; yet

> the fog was where I wanted to be. . . . Everything looked and sounded unreal. Nothing was what it is. That's what I wanted—to be alone with myself in another world where truth is untrue and life can hide from itself.

For Edmund, darkness connotes alienation and unbearable hurt but also the illusion of concord, perfect "peace." He inhabits this unstable world knowingly, but Mary cannot "understand" its complexity, its multiple connotations. She always returns to her intolerance of the gross, unpredictable happenings and discomforts that intrude upon her wishful fantasy of blissful security. Yet her defensive maneuvers cannot banish the "dark" implications shared by light. So she commutes between her notions of paradise without pain—uncontaminated light--and hell without redemption—unrelieved darkness--irrevocably and pointlessly suspended, like Hamlet, between enigmatic images.

Beckett's images in *Waiting for Godot*, like those alluded to by O'Neill, mirror the paradoxical, inseparable, convertible natures of constancy and its anomalous nemesis. Didi and Gogo, like Edmund in *Long Day's Journey* and Job, accept the bewildering exchange, avoiding Hamlet's and Mary Tyrone's perpetual fluctuation between simplified contraries. His two brave characters face metaphorical duality, but like Edmund they are willing to tolerate negative as well as affirmative connotations, both the distressing abnormalities and comforting constants, as a path to adaptation. They realize that darkness (like light) is fluid, two-faced, and therefore difficult but necessary to fathom.

On one hand, it offers the finality of peace that Mary Tyrone sought. The day's end, after a rapid, unhappy journey, at last closes down upsetting encounters, a necessary release. "The hours are long," Didi speculates, filled with unclear "proceedings" that may not "prevent our reason from foundering," so besides waiting for Godot, they wait "for night to fall." Darkness provides respite from the daytime "suffering." "We have struggled, unassisted. Now it's over." Pozzo describes the twilight "lyrically" as a "veil of gentleness and peace," and Didi welcomes it: "it is not for nothing I have lived through this long day and I can assure you it is very near the end of its repertory."

Simplicity and Irony

On the other hand, Pozzo comments, night harbors a multitude of unknowns. It may copy the finality of death:

> One day we were born, one day we shall die, the same day, the same second, is that not enough for you? They give birth astride of a grave, the light gleams an instant, then it's night once more.

Or, if not oblivion, night can bring on a "private nightmare," its "abyssal depths" harboring irrational beatings, health problems, upsetting dreams, "straying in the night without end," and confrontation with "nothingness" ("We are all born mad. Some remain so"). Its coming may be anticipated as a comforting constant, but its consequences, like those brought on by day, are unpredictable.

Didi and Gogo struggle to realize an adaptation that might integrate permanence and transience, or consistency with deviation. In traditional style, while the forlorn landscape reflects their occasional despair, a leafing tree reflects their intermittent hope. However, the images of light and darkness cannot reflect a definitive solution as long as each represents *both* sides of a fluid, unstable predicament.

Similarly, the self-contradictions connoted by light and darkness in *Long Day's Journey* reveal an unresolved antithesis between good will and a failure to forgive or at least tolerate others without lapsing into depression, blaming, and perplexity. Thoughtful writers as diverse as Beckett and O'Neill, Shakespeare and Matthew, Aeschylus and Seneca, Nietzsche and Darwin have visualized and proposed remedies for that frustrating paradox, but its authority remains intact, a persistent universal dilemma.

8
The Genius of Joseph Conrad

A Master of Metaphor

In addition to his remarkable narrative and rhetorical virtuosity, Joseph Conrad was a master of metaphor. Every visual and auditory reference in his novels and short stories implies (corresponds to) an emotional or ethical condition. Sensory allusions do not merely clarify the author's vision; they embody it. They objectify feelings and thoughts associated with desperate ordeals, trials of manhood. Conrad transformed the sounds and sights of arduous adventures (many derived from his own experience) into a dream world where ordinary façades conveyed extraordinary issues.

"There are those voyages that seem ordered for the illustration of life," Marlow observes in "Youth" (1902) "that might stand for a symbol of existence." Some characters are immune to that symbolism: in "Typhoon," the literal-minded Captain MacWhirr "expostulated against the use of images in speech." The language of metaphor was to him a foreign tongue. But the hopeful commander in *The Shadow-Line* sees his ship as an emblem revealing an "illusion of life and character."

"Common everyday words," the narrator asserts in *Heart of Darkness*, "had behind them, to my mind, the terrific suggestiveness of words heard in dreams, of phrases spoken in nightmares." "Common everyday" images construct the metaphorical foundation of Conrad's stories—a matchbox in "Typhoon" ("his fingers closed again on the small object as though it had been the symbol of all these little habits that chain us to the weary round of life"), a house of cards in *An Outcast of the Islands*.

Familiar objects or experiences evoke tiresome habits, impulsive acts, persistent perplexities, cataclysmic confrontations, and awesome defeats. Conrad's ventures and routines at sea or in tropical forests and trading posts served as sources of imagery far more prominent and supportive than the sparse urban settings in later "political" novels like *The Secret Agent* and *Under Western Eyes*.

In "Karain," a prosaic setting becomes linked to grand "illusions." The warrior chief parades extravagant ideas advertising his "manliness" to a receptive audience as if the small cabin in a schooner were a stage for him to perform for the world. He re-enacts a colorful but futile daily show to reassert his lost status. Karain might be only "the master of an insignificant foothold" in a remote tropical village, but "he presented himself essentially as an actor, as a human being aggressively disguised." The theater metaphor conjures up the impressiveness but also the artificiality of his performance.

In *Almayer's Folly*, grubby eating utensils—"a cracked glass tumbler and a tin spoon" sitting on a table alongside "a plateful of rice and fish, a jar of water and a bottle half full of genever"—underline the pathos of unfulfilled "dreams":

> In his mind's eye he saw the rich prize in his grasp; and, with tin spoon in his hand, he was forgetting the plateful of rice before him in the fanciful arrangement of some splendid banquet to take place on his arrival in Amsterdam.

Other tawdry images contradict Almayer's impotent fixation on opulence just as obviously. In two houses—one "shabby" and decrepit, the other new but unfinished—the dreamer of shabby, unfinished enterprises waits "endlessly" for financial fruition. He imagines "crowning all, in the far future, . . . a fairy palace, the big mansion in Amsterdam, that earthly paradise of his dreams," a palace built for "indolent ease" and "inexpressible splendor," so different from the "sadly decaying" house that Captain Lingard erected for him two decades earlier, now in disrepair with its dusty office, broken furniture littering the dirty main room, and "many withered plants and dried earth scattered about. A general air of squalid neglect pervaded the place."

> He killed time wandering sadly in the overgrown paths round the house . . . [where] only a few broken cases of moldering Manchester goods reminded him of the good early times when all this was full of life and merchandise.

Nina accepts "without question or apparent disgust the neglect, decay, and poverty of the household, the absence of furniture, and the preponderance of rice diet on the family table." When she escapes with Dain, the author diligently explains why the offended father burns down the place:

> Certain things had to be taken out of his life, stamped out of sight, destroyed, forgotten. . . . The desk, the paper, the torn books, and the broken shelves, all under a thick coat of dust. The very dust and bones of a dead and gone business.

> As time went on the grass grew over the black patch of ground where the old house used to stand, and nothing remained to mark the place of the dwelling that had sheltered

Almayer's young hopes, his foolish dream of splendid future, his awakening, and his despair.

Conrad was just as explicit in regard to the half-finished new house, "new but already decaying—that last failure of his life." Dutch naval officers name it, appropriately, "Almayer's Folly." The mercurial trader had begun construction with short-lived enthusiasm for a recovery of "great fortunes for himself and Nina," until his hopes typically came to nothing in "the great empty rooms where the tepid wind entering through the sashless windows whirled gently the dried leaves and the dust of many days of neglect."

Now he finds "refuge" and "solitude" in the big dusty rooms. After destroying the older house, he had walked

> slowly away from the fire towards the shelter of "Almayer's Folly." In that manner did Almayer move into his new house. He took possession of the new ruin, and in the undying folly of his heart set himself to wait in anxiety and pain for that forgetfulness which was slow to come. He had done all he could.

He acquires a fitting housemate, a Chinese opium addict who renames their refuge, ironically, "House of heavenly delight." Almayer dies there, finally "delivered from the trammels of his earthly folly."

Fiction "appeals primarily to the senses," and Conrad tried "to make you *hear*" as well as "to make you see" (Preface, *The Nigger of the "Narcissus"*). His auditory references, while not nearly as frequent or elaborate as the visual imagery, can be quite telling. Noise contributes to the discordant ambiance produced by a world out of joint, and the *absence* of sound also can connote desolation:

> On Lingard's departure, solitude and silence closed round Willems; the cruel solitude of one abandoned by men; the reproachful silence which surrounds an outcast ejected by his kind, the silence unbroken by the slightest whisper of hope; an immense and impenetrable silence that swallows without echo the murmur of regret and the cry of revolt. (*Outcast*)

Consistent with the interplay of emotional or moral contraries, disquieting silence often alternates with disquieting sound:

> A scream, unexpected, piercing—a scream beginning at once in the highest pitch of a woman's voice and then cut short, so short that it suggested the swift work of death—caused Ali to jump on one side away from the hammock, and the silence that succeeded seemed to him as startling as the awful shriek. (*Outcast*)

In "Typhoon" the contrast between frightening noise and its sudden absence ends benignly. At first the din seems overwhelming. The storm batters Captain MacWhirr's ship with a "confused clamor" that was "tumultuous and very loud—made up of the rush of the wind, the crashes of the sea, with that prolonged deep vibration of the air, like the roll of an immense and remote drum beating the charge of the gale." A "great physical tumult" deafens the officers and brings

> a profound trouble to their souls. One of those wild and appalling shrieks that are heard at times passing mysteriously overhead in the steady roar of a hurricane,

swooped, as if borne on wings, upon the ship. . . . A loud and wild resonance, made up of all the noises of the hurricane, dwelt in the still warmth of the air.

In addition to the "swirling, raving tumult" of the storm, "two hundred Chinese coolies" create

a tumult of strangled, throaty shrieks that produced an effect of desperate confusion, . . . a confused uproar, a tempestuous tumult, a fierce mutter, gusts of screams dying away, and the tramping of feet mingling with the blows of the sea.

Contradicting the "tumult," MacWhirr's voice seems "forced and ringing feebly, but with a penetrating effect of quietness in the enormous discord of noises." It is a "frail and indomitable sound," a "dwarf sound" that stays "unconquered in the giant tumult." That "small, lonely and unmoved" voice commands other sailors to reinstitute order; "it seemed to Jukes . . . that [the captain] had overcome the wind somehow; that a silence had fallen upon the ship, a silence in which the sea struck thunderously at her sides." He was able to hear "small sounds that seemed to have survived the great uproar."

Again in *Outcast*, noise and quiet alternate in a storm that registers Lingard's militancy, Aïssa's "bewilderment," and Willems' defensiveness. An absence of sound signals the prefatory stage:

The sullen silence of the earth [was] oppressed by the aspect of coming turmoil, the silence of the world collecting its faculties to withstand the storm. . . . She started, watched every word on his lips, and after he finished speaking she remained still and mute in astonished immobility.

As Lingard's rage and Willems' pathetic rejoinders increase or decrease in intensity, the volume of sound fluctuates inconclusively, no longer a stable harbinger of either "joy" (*Shadow-Line*) or fear ("Typhoon"):

> Willems' voice filled the enclosure, rising louder with every word, and then, suddenly, at its very loudest, stopped short—as water stops running from an overturned vessel. As soon as it had ceased the thunder seemed to take up the burden in a low growl coming from the inland hills.
> The noise approached in confused mutterings which kept on increasing, swelling into a roar that came nearer, rushed down the river, passed close in a tearing crash—and instantly sounded faint, dying away in monotonous and dull repetitions amongst the endless sinuosities of the lower reaches.
>
> The silence, that had rushed in on the track of the passing tumult, remained suspended as deep and complete as if it had never been disturbed from the beginning of remote ages.
>
> They were deafened by a near, single crash of thunder, which was followed by a rushing noise, like a frightened sigh of the startled earth. . . . Their voices, after the deep and tremendous noise, sounded to them very unsat-

isfactory—thin and frail, like the voices of pigmies—and they became suddenly silent.

Finally, Willems and Aïssa, banished by the captain, walk away quietly in a violent downpour, concluding the confused interplay of contrasting moods. Vacillation between deafening and muted sounds has replicated human ambivalence.

The Shadow-Line mixes noise with a despairing, silent "immobility." The silence of a "dead calm," not a deafening uproar, delivers the threat of chaos and death, tumult associated now with salvation. "There was not a sound," and

> a great over-heated stillness enveloped the ship and seemed to hold her motionless.

> For a long, long time I faced an empty world, steeped in an infinity of silence. . . . The intense loneliness of the sea acted like poison on my brain.

> The brooding stillness of the world seemed sensitive to the slightest sound like a whispering gallery. . . . The terrible thing was that the only voice that I ever heard was my own.

> Perfect silence, joined to perfect immobility, proclaimed the yet unbroken spell of our helplessness.

"Everything's so still that one might think everybody in the ship was dead," Mr. Burns grumbles. The captain's orders are met with a "silence which followed upon my words [that] was almost harder to bear than the angriest uproar. I was crushed by the infinite depth of its reproach." But at last, with the onset of a breeze, "the barrier of awful stillness which had encompassed us for so many days as though we had been accursed was broken. . . . The wind sang in a strenuous note which under other circumstances would have expressed to me all the joy of life."

Conrad undoubtedly observed the play of auditory contraries in Baudelaire, from whose short poem "La Musique," published in *Les Fleurs du mal* in 1857, he extracted an epigraph for *The Shadow-Line*: "D'autres fois, calme plat, grand miroir / De mon désespoir." "La Musique" in prose translation by Francis Scarfe:

> Music often sweeps me away like a sea, and under a canopy of mist or through the vast ether, I set sail for my faint star.
>
> Breasting the swell, with my lungs dilated like a ship's canvas, I ride up the backs of the piled waves which the darkness veils from me;
>
> I feel all the passions of a groaning ship vibrate within me; the fair wind and the tempest's rage
>
> Cradle me on the fathomless deep—or else there is a flat calm, the giant mirror of my despair.

Music can evoke sounds and silences that correspond to the contrasting emotions of the auditor.

In Conrad's dream world, however, pictorial images take precedence over auditory images. Nature's most "common everyday" visual facts, light and darkness—the pairing so popular in biblical, Greek, and Roman literature—became the author's chief metaphorical reference. Conrad wished to "compel men entranced by the sight of distant goals to glance for a moment at the surrounding vision of form and color, of sunshine and shadows" (Preface, *The Nigger of the "Narcissus"*). "Sunshine gleams between the lines of those short paragraphs," the captain says in "Karain"—"sunshine and the glitter of the sea."

Darkness Versus Light

Conrad orchestrated the figurative coupling of "sunshine and shadows" to visualize an age-old rivalry between life and death. In literary works from the Bible and Greek drama down to the present, life force becomes associated with noble principles and practices while life denial becomes equivalent to moral surrender. Masculine virtue ("in action how like an angel," in Hamlet's words, "in apprehension how like a god") opposes irrational or ignoble conduct. "Manly" qualities such as unyielding courage, agile leadership, immovable equanimity, and nautical skill duel with fear, illness, mindless violence, ignorance, immorality, and death.

Their combat can be projected tangibly and simply, as it was by Jesus, with simple characters clearly identifiable as either good or evil, or it can be conveyed by complex characters who embody the internal convergence of those conflicting orientations. Conrad dealt with both types.

Among his protagonists, one was staunchly affirmative—the old-fashioned, stereotypical hero, exemplar of masculine strength who maintains his poise during a fearful trial. This figure, visualized in "Typhoon," "The Secret Sharer," and *The Shadow-Line,* was a favorite of Conrad's predecessors like Jules Verne and dominated adventure literature at the time. Ethical constancy was its strength and salvation. But the character could be one-dimensional, even monotonous, and precludes the possibility of tragic suspension between contrary positions. Although depicting stereotypical success may be a valid literary enterprise, it did not inspire Conrad's most original writing.

At the other ethical extreme, Conrad's protagonists may dramatize the total *absence* of ideal virtue. Almayer in *Almayer's Folly* (1895), Verloc in *The Secret Agent* (1907), and Heyst in *Victory* (1915) lack elevated values. They too, like heroic exemplars, do not internalize a convergence of noble commitment and ignoble betrayal. Instead they identify with personal whim, financial gain, political intrigue, or stoic detachment.

That limitation denies them the complexity elicited by tragic polarity, but a morally limited identity can sometimes be transformed. Romantic obsession converts Heyst, the "universal detached man," to "hope, to love—and to put [his] trust in life!" He forfeits his monolithic isolation and gains "a greater sense of his own reality than he had ever known in all his life."

Some of Conrad's most interesting characters, in fact, are neither wholly "heroic" nor ignoble. They fluctuate between incompatible outlooks; they adopt negative positions while recalling or imagining glorious ventures: ethical negativity alternates with ethical affirmation. Karain oscillates between disgrace and reassertion. Willems in *Outcast* nurtures a strange package of avarice, sexual urgency, and "settled conceptions of respectable conduct."

And the insightful narrator in "Youth" contrasts the enthusiasm of youth with the cynicism of age. He voices an ongoing regret for lost potency, remembering defeat and bad luck while generalizing about his high-spirited "tempestuous passions" in earlier years:

> Oh, the glamour of youth! Oh, the fire of it, more dazzling than the flames of the burning ship, throwing a magic light on the wide earth, leaping audaciously to the sky, presently to be quenched by time, more cruel, more piti-

less, more bitter than the sea—and like the flames of the burning ship surrounded by an impenetrable night.

"All the love of loot and the love of glory," Conrad wrote, "the love of adventure and the love of danger, with the great love of the unknown and vast dreams of dominion and power, have passed like images reflected from a mirror" (*The Mirror of the Sea*, 1906).]

When Conrad casts the competition between life affirmation and denial as a war between ethical integrity and dishonor, "a taint of death" infects the "commonplace" images of light and darkness.

The first novel, *Almayer's Folly*, begins optimistically. Light connotes exuberant energy, high hopes, and elevated principles. The forest embodies vibrant energy, its "plants shooting upward, entwined, interlaced in extricable confusion, climbing madly and brutally over each other in the terrible silence of a desperate struggle towards the life-giving sunshine above." Taminah "lived like the tall palms amongst which she was passing now, seeking the light, desiring the sunshine, fearing the storm, unconscious of either."

But night submerges vitality and decency. It introduces despair, stagnation, decay, death. After Dain parts from Nina "the sun dipped sharply, as if ashamed of being detected in a sympathizing attitude, and the clearing, which during the day was all light, became suddenly all darkness." "Would a man willingly remain long in a dark place?" Dain asks; "What is life to me without light?" So he runs off with Nina "in the crude blaze of the vertical sun, in that light violent and vibrating, like a triumphal flourish of brazen trumpets." Nina "stood in full light, framed in the dark background," becoming surrounded by "a ruddy halo of light shining through the black and odorous smoke."

Yet darkness constantly imperils light:

> The sun shone with that dazzling light in which her love was born and grew till it possessed her whole being. . . . [But] the short tropical twilight went out before she could draw the long breath of relief; and now the sudden darkness seemed to be full of menacing voices calling upon her to rush headlong into the unknown.

> A heavy thunder-cloud had crept down from the hills blotting out the stars, merging sky, forest, and river into one mass of almost palpable blackness.

The peril of darkness threatens Almayer's practical attitude toward money as well as Dain's and Nina's romance. Processing all information in terms of wealth or poverty, Almayer as a young man "was gifted with a strong and active imagination, and . . . he saw, as in a flash of dazzling light, great piles of shining guilders." Darkness concealed no danger then: "the smooth black surface of the sea [had] a great bar of gold laid on it by the rising moon."

But at present, "it was too dark to distinguish anything," and he finally glimpses the issue. "It seemed to him that for many years he had been falling into a deep precipice": it was a smooth, round, black thing, and the black walls had been rushing upwards with wearisome rapidity. Every outline had disappeared in the intense blackness that seemed to have destroyed everything but space. Only the fire glimmered like a star forgotten in this annihilation of all visible things.

As Marlow discovers in "Youth," light always reappears and darkness always overruns it. "The masts fell just before daybreak, and for a moment there was a burst and turmoil of sparks that seemed to fill with flying fire the night patient and watchful, the vast night lying silent upon the sea." The crew of the Judea hopefully pours water into its burning ship but "the bright stream flashed in sunshine, fell into a layer of white crawling smoke, and vanished on the black surface of coal."

Twenty-two years later, Marlow remembers his first sight of the East, "a flick of sunshine upon a strange shore": "the semicircle of a beach gleamed faintly, like an illusion. There was not a light, not a stir, not a sound. The mysterious East faced me, perfumed like a flower, silent like death, dark like a grave."

In "Karain," darkness dominates "a land where nothing could survive the coming of the night, and where each sunrise, like a dazzling act of special creation, was disconnected from the eve and the morrow." Night, occasionally heralded by weird thunder and lightning, is depressing, a suitable time for madness, regret, recrimination. Starlight, a "signal fire," a "line of white surf" offer little consolation; even "the glittering confusion of stars resembled a mad turmoil."

In "Typhoon" (1902), although the protagonist maintains his courage, darkness swallows light. The engineer of the Nan-Shan "dropped into the dark hole with a whoop," and the sun too drops into a "sinister dark" cloud that encompasses the ship. The stars "took flight together and disappeared, leaving only a blackness flecked with white flashes, for the sea was as black as the sky." Without the reassuring guidance of stars, Jukes reflects, "the far-off blackness ahead of the ship was like another night seen through the starry night of the earth—the starless night of the immensities beyond the created universe."

Darkness associates with noise: "the gale howled and scuffled about gigantically in the darkness, as though the entire world were one black gully." In the midst of violence, "a light to get drowned by" supplies the only illumination as "the whole black universe seemed to reel together with the ship." The efforts of the seamen seem as futile as "the last star [that] struggled with the colossal depth of blackness hanging over the ship—and went out. . . . The darkness was absolutely piling itself upon the ship."

Light puts up strenuous resistance. The intrepid captain, avatar of manly virtue, maintains his composure despite (or thanks to) his limited intellectual and imaginative capacity, his failure to comprehend the psychological threat as well as the physical danger assaulting his crew. The "small" voice of MacWhirr, "lonely and unmoved," speaks out "in the solitude and the pitch darkness," resisting the blackness and uproar of the hurricane ("do or die").

MacWhirr and Jukes manage to impose a degree of order, their fortitude as implacable and mindless as the typhoon's violence. It is marked by a sudden glimpse of light—a "patch of glittering sky" and the "splendor" of a few stars--and the men survive. The ship "rumbled in her depths, shaking a white plummet of steam into the night."

The correspondence between image and import is unmistakable, the allegory quite obvious. No matter how puny and overmatched, light remains stubbornly inextinguishable; darkness may menace a brave seaman, yet he escapes shameful reactions.

Nevertheless, the love of glory or loot usually becomes "quenched" by time and adversity. Or else it is contaminated; Conrad explored that outcome in "The Lagoon" and "Karain" (both 1897), forerunners of *Heart of Darkness* (1899), *Lord Jim* (1900), and *Nostromo* (1904). He goes beyond metaphorical rivalry and introduces a Jobian subversion of sunshine. As in the Book of Job and the *Oresteia* of Aeschylus, light reverses its traditional connotations and becomes a corrupted agent of darkness while continuing to refer to its former positive identity. The two connotations take turns!

Karain illustrates that fluctuation in metaphorical detail. Sunshine cannot redeem his crime; it no longer offers unqualified support or consolation. It has been transformed, not defeated as in "Youth" or overwhelmed as in "Typhoon." Now it imitates its old enemy, pitiless and disorienting. It has become as dishonorable as the protagonist.

Like Marlow in "Youth," Karain tries to resurrect his preeminence in the sun. Daylight allows him to play a stage role portraying courage, martial prowess, loyalty, and wise leadership; each day, in dazzling sunshine, he resurrects his "dream" of "barbarous dignity," always "faithful to the illusions of the stage." "The sun blazed down into a shadowless hollow of colors and stillness" and "the bay was like a bottomless pit of intense light": in that brilliant illumination, Karain's staged "mysteries" rebut his treason, buttress his role as charismatic ruler, and rehabilitate his questionable history.

The daily performance of mighty manhood, however, turns out to be "empty," not "wonderful," only a misleading "glimmer" that fitfully conceals disgrace, "failure, and death." "At sunset the night descended upon him quickly, like a falling curtain." Karain murdered his ally in the sunshine, which "fell on my back colder than the running water." That fact refutes his performance as a "resplendent" actor, and when his listeners realize that "this is not a play," he "seemed to wake up from a dream."

The magic charm devised by Hollis saves him "from the fear of outer darkness," allowing him to re-enter his magnificent dream theater. "He left us, and seemed straightway to step into the glorious splendor of his stage, to wrap himself in the illusion of unavoidable success." But he cannot escape "a taint of death."

The Dissolution of Identity

In Conrad's most significant writing, *compromised* integrity, commuting between respectable reputation and disreputable memories, evolves into *dissolved* integrity. The author tells a unique story: a character of admirable aspiration and limited intelligence commits a major error of judgment and turns into a walking enigma who does not simply alternate between high principle and bad conscience but creates a morbid union of the two.

When this character sacrifices integrity with some perverse act he sacrifices clarity as well as self-respect and safety. Once self-righteous and invulnerable, he wanders in a cloud of confusion and regret, self-abasement and false hope, unable to answer the sacred question, What am I? He lapses into a profound moral void.

Like the tragic hero, he betrays his reputation, but his predicament is not clear-cut and predictable, not a recognizable suspension between grace and dishonor. He becomes mired in an obscure muddle. He imagines he is as "solid as the hills," yet shows himself to be as insubstantial as "fragments of night floating on moonbeams." Conrad's novels and short works reveal an increasing inclination to elaborate, sometimes in abstract terms, the idea of personality dissolution. "I am nothing," Nostromo mutters. No, he is something, something twisted and incomprehensible, "remarkable" yet "mysterious." That mystery captivated Conrad's imagination.

In conventional usage, light retains its physical appearance whether serving as a positive or negative force in the metaphors of moral rivalry and corruption. It may triumph, suffer defeat, or become converted, but its sensory manifestation stays constant. It illuminates, it is bright.

Conrad's account of muddled identity changes this expectation. Light forfeits its usual appearance, surrenders its sensory integrity, and merges with its visual contradiction. They come together in an amorphous synthesis, a baffling conjunction of contraries. They mingle their physical properties along with their contrasting ethical implications in a single muddled image that projects an unearthly meaning.

No longer does darkness simply oppose or pervert light. They cohabit in a "somber" environment where one gets "lost amongst shapeless things that were dangerous and ghastly" (*Outcast*). In his innovative writing, Conrad associated that cohabitation with shadows, mist, and gloom to indicate the "inconclusive" fusion of moral assertion and denial. A mystifying mingling of "sunshine and shadows" reflected incoherence, variability, and instability. Traditional pictorial boundaries coalesced to form a garbled, perplexing mixture.

Unlike the readily understood rivalry delineated by Jesus, the carefully explained inversions in the Book of Job, or the well-defined reversals endured by Mary and Edmund Tyrone and by Gogo and Didi, this extraordinary metaphor is not sharply demarcated either in physical form or moral import. Its indistinct outlines forfeit easy identification and embody the incongruity that plagues vacillating, disoriented, largely inarticulate characters. It symbolizes their uncertainty—their indeterminate status.

The conception of imagery as a vehicle to project a jumbled, unstable simultaneity of righteous aspiration and degraded conduct intrigued and challenged the author. It became his "emblematic" signature. It first appeared some twenty years after Nietzsche declared the succession of disparate identities and about the same time that Egon Schiele and other artists were exploring abnormal figurations. Nietzsche, Schiele, and Conrad understood how grotesque images could "shelter" unstable identities.

Conrad suggested a weird fusion of contrary metaphors in his first novel, *Almayer's Folly* (1895). Darkness does not only contest, nullify, transform, or alternate with light; they merge to form an inconstant and unrecognizable mutant "born in gloom." A "red glare" or a "crimson glow" veils objects "in the play of light and shadow" as a "gray shadow descended upon the land." Babalatchi "stopped for a while in . . . black patches of shadow," and Dain leaves Nina in a boat looming large in the full light of the moon, a black shapeless mass in the slight haze hanging over the water. . . . In a little while all the outlines got blurred, confused, and soon disappeared in the folds of white vapor shrouding the middle of the river.

Slow-witted Almayer is enveloped by shadows when "the harsh brilliance of the lamp was toned above into a soft half-light that lost itself in the obscurity amongst the rafters," while in the "dim light twinkling through bamboo walls, a smoky torch [was] burning on the platforms built out over the river." But the shallow, unimaginative hero remains unaware of the implications carried by these images. He cannot perceive their complexity or force. He sees no significance in a bizarre forest, whose "outlines wavered, grew thin, dissolved in the air."

And he sleeps while casting a gross yet insubstantial silhouette on a wall:

> In the increasing light of the moon that had risen now above the night mist, the objects on the verandah came out strongly outlined in black splashes of shadow with all the uncompromising ugliness of their disorder, and a caricature of the sleeping Almayer appeared on the dirty whitewash of the wall behind him in a grotesquely exag-

gerated detail of attitude and feature enlarged to a heroic size.

Revelatory passages like this, anticipating Willems' shadow play at the outset of *Outcast*, outline perplexing, distorted flux rather than clearly outlined combat, corruption, or alternation.

Not entirely confident in his first novel, the author would sometimes feel compelled to point out the significance of his images as they became increasingly murky. Since the imperceptive protagonist hardly realizes how shadowy appearances mirror his amorphous mental state, the author must explain:

> Almayer looked vainly westward for a ray of light out of the gloom of his shattered hopes.

> The decision issued from the fog-veiled offices of the Borneo Company darkened for Almayer the brilliant sunshine of the Tropics, and added another drop of bitterness to the cup of his disenchantments.

An Outcast of the Islands (1896) develops the technique of identity diffusion more fully but just as explicitly, as light and its contradiction fuse in "shadowy" proximity to shape an inexplicable alliance. They have conjoined, rendering moral vision unreliable and "full of unexpected surprises." Conrad makes abundantly concrete his chief character's dream-like metamorphosis into "fragments of night floating on moon-beams."

Initially, the imagery seems to suit immovable, unimaginative vanity. Willems can sense no challenge to integrity, no impending transformation; his self-adulation is satisfying, predictable, untroubled:

> He imagined that he could go on afterwards looking at the sunshine, enjoying the shade . . . . He was unable to conceive that the moral significance of any act of his . . . could dim the light of the sun.
> Willems had the street to himself. He would walk in the middle, his shadow gliding obsequiously before him. He looked down on it complacently. The shadow of a successful man!

The image, of course, is an ironic one; Conrad's sarcasm hints at an impending transition from sunshine to obscurity. The "shadow of a successful man," lacking substance and constancy, will be Willems' hallmark.

Willems "imagines" moral belief as the triumph of light over darkness. During his humiliation in Macasser, he briefly suspects a negative outcome when night becomes "more vast and more black." "For a time he came out of himself, out of his selfishness—out of the constant preoccupation of his interests and his desires—out of the temple of self." The binnacle lamps on Lingard's ship cast "a circle of light" in the blackness, and Willems, standing in "the gleam of the light" with his fatherly savior, once again "reveled in the extreme purity of his heart . . . [and] the praiseworthy solidity of his principles."

But his self-justification and "preoccupation" with money reappear after the upright Captain Lingard salvages his dignity. Since he cannot conceive that his guiding principles lack solidity, he fits Babalatchi's description of blind old Omar: "it was written when he was born that he should end his life in darkness, and now he is like a man walking in a black night—with his eyes open, yet seeing not." Aware of "the unstable nature of earthly greatness," the one-eyed Babalatchi wisely recognizes existence as an intense but temporary point of light whose "fierce animation"--a "short-lived flame"-- quickly dies.

Or light may not be extinguished but instead become destructive after an unholy conversion. Sunshine—"brilliant, crude, heavy, lying on a dead land like a pall of fire"—can blight instead of nurture, just as Willems' dream of wealth and status, a "vision of dazzling glory," promotes corruption.

> The land lay silent, still, and brilliant under the avalanche of burning rays that had destroyed all sound and all motion, had buried all shadows, had choked every breath. No living thing dared to affront the serenity of this cloudless sky, dared to revolt against the oppression of this glorious and cruel sunshine.

"The intensity of that tropical life, . . . which seems to be all grace of color and form, all brilliance, all smiles," Conrad writes, "is only the blossoming of the dead; [its] mystery holds the promise of joy and beauty, yet contains nothing but poison and decay."

Even more disconcerting and surprising, light and its contradiction come together in "shadowy" proximity to form an inexplicable alliance, the ultimate paradox. Willems, guided by Aïssa, enters an alien landscape where no identity can be permanently fixed as either defeated or victorious, subordinate or dominant, lion-hearted or apathetic; instead it takes on a fleeting, indefinable, appalling fluidity:

> Willems saw a flash of white and color, a gleam of gold like a sun-ray lost in shadow, and a vision of blackness darker than the deepest shade of the forest.

> He had a notion of being lost amongst shapeless things that were dangerous and ghastly.

Events often take place in the flickering shadows of campfires: "the forms by the fire moved; the shadow of the woman altered its shape." "Torches blaze, sending out much more smoke than light." Omar's "sightless face was plain one second, blurred the next in the play of the light . . .. With its shifting lights and shadows, [it] let out nothing." Willems' eyes "glittered deep down in the sockets like the last sparks amongst the black embers of a burnt-out fire." Every object or occurrence, sometimes in conjunction with muted sounds, donates a half-lit threatening uncertainty.

> It was a somber creek of black water speckled with the gold of scattered sunlight falling through the boughs that met overhead in a soaring, restless arc full of gentle whispers passing, tremulous, aloft amongst the thick leaves.

Ethical and emotional disarray accompany the visual and auditory obscurity. Submerged in a nebulous, "blurred," "ill-defined" pool of motives, engulfed in "silence, cold, mournful, profound, more like death than peace"—a "stillness perfect and absolute"—he "sought refuge within his ideas of propriety from the dismal mangroves, from the darkness of the forests." Were those ideas only a lovely "dream," he wonders, or an "infamous nightmare"? Light and dark have conjoined, making both material motives and moral vision untrustworthy and "full of unexpected surprises." Conrad weds pictorial extravagance with analytic precision to make tangible his characters' dreamlike dissolution into "fragments of night floating on moonbeams."

Aïssa, her dim shape set against a dim background, seems as shadowy as the dark portraits—the chiaroscuro—of Leonardo or Rembrandt. She is like "the animated and brilliant flower of all that exuberant life which, born in gloom, struggles forever towards the sunshine," at once overpoweringly sensuous and ethereal. In the unsteady light, her eyes seem "somber and gleaming like a starry night." She appears to Lingard "as if she had been made . . . out of the black vapors of the sky and of the sinister gleams of feeble sunshine."

In Willems' muddy imagination, she blends delight with jeopardy to yield an unfathomable result. He cannot comprehend, resist, or assimilate her "indistinct and vague" yet compelling appeal. This shadowy female changes a white man into a "colorless" nonentity.

> Through the checkered light between them she appeared to him with the impalpable distinctness of a dream. The very spirit of that land of mysterious forests, standing before him like an apparition behind a transparent veil—a veil woven of sunbeams and shadows.

Conrad repeats the "enigma" relentlessly. "All through the languid stillness of that night [Willems] fought with the impalpable; he fought with the shadows, with the darkness, with the silence." The faltering trader cannot resolve his ordeal:

> A veil of motionless cloud . . . with its masses of black and grey seemed to chase the light with wicked intent, and with an ominous and gloomy steadiness, as though con-

scious of the message of violence and turmoil they carried. At the sun's disappearance below the western horizon, the immense cloud, in quickened motion, grappled with the glow of retreating light, . . . undecided—as if brooding over its own power for good or for evil.

Willems can hardly "distinguish the various degrees of formless blackness"; even familiar household objects are "lost in shadow" or ominously masked by smoke.

> The long barrel of a gun leaning against the chest caught the stray rays of the smoky illumination in trembling gleams that wavered, disappeared, reappeared, went out, came back—as if engaged in a doubtful struggle with the darkness that, lying in wait in distant corners, seemed to dart out viciously towards its feeble enemy . . . . Muffled-up human shapes hovered for a moment near the edge of light and retreated suddenly back into the darkness.

If Willems, himself a "muffled-up human shape," is a paradox to himself, he is also one to Aïssa and Lingard. He had appeared to Aïssa shining with a blinding, ruinous light "as brilliant, as terrible, as necessary, as the sun that gives life to these lands: the sun of unclouded skies that dazzles and withers; the sun beneficent and wicked—the giver of light, perfume, and pestilence." But she sinks into "profound" bewilderment when that sunlight "seemed traversed by ghastly flashes of uncertain darkness."

Lingard finds Willems just as indecipherable. Staunchly defending a gentleman's code of conduct, the captain hopes that "a ray of light would shoot through the thick blackness of inexplicable treachery." Yet he never sees through the "cloud of smoke" obscuring his disciple. "I can see nothing," he protests; "it's too dark."

When Lingard's "notions of justice"—until then "preordained and unchangeable"—give way to doubt and disgust, "the smooth darkness filling the shutter-hole grew paler and became blotchy with ill-defined shapes, as if a new universe was being evolved out of somber chaos." The day, "dismal and oppressed by the fog of the river and by the heavy vapors of the sky," appears "without color and without sunshine: incomplete, disappointing, and sad," while "under the grey motionless waste of a stormy sky, drifted low black vapors, in stretching bars, in shapeless patches, in sinuous wisps and tormented spirals."

Lingard seeks "the clear effect of a simple cause," yet his ward's "inexplicable treachery" baffles him. In his mind, Willems has become a symbolic carrier of "some immense infamy—of something vague, disgusting and terrible, . . . a floating and unsteady mist in human shape." "You are neither white nor brown," he exclaims, "you have no color as you have no heart. . . . You are a bitter thought, a something without a body and that must be hidden. . . . You are my shame."

After his convoluted journey in shadow land, Willems, at the moment of death, tries to reach through the fog ("foggy nights spent in the bush will soon break the strongest backs," Almayer had commented), groping without success toward illumination, "the triumphant delight of sunshine and of life." Appropriately, Lingard buries his fogbound disciple in a hill where darkness meets light, "a black, rounded mass upon the silver paleness of the sky." Years later, a drunken naturalist underlines the irony of Willems' career by mistranslating the Latin inscription on the trader's gravestone: "Don't waste your breath in abusing shadows."

"The Lagoon" develops this relationship between metaphorical and moral dissolution. Conrad begins the story in orthodox fashion, opposing the vitality of sunshine with the decay of grim night. Just before sunset, the "intense glitter" of a "dazzling" sun cuts a path through the "somber and dull" forest, before being submerged by "the darkness, mysterious and invincible; the darkness scented and poisonous of impenetrable forests."

Quickly, however, light gets "filled with gloom," not opposed to or converted by its rival but interwoven with it. Locations that "harbor both light and darkness" encompass a "vague" reality that differs from either conflict or inversion. "Distorted shadows" or "breathless shadows" take precedence and replace "the enormous conflagration of sunset." "Black stillness" joins rather than co-opts the "glitter of stars," their separate and distinct identities merging in a "shapeless" arena of torment, and fog takes over an unearthly country:

> The earth enfolded in the starlight peace became a shadowy country of inhuman strife, a battle-field of phantoms terrible and charming, august or ignoble, struggling ardently for the possession of our helpless hearts.

Fog takes over this country as "over the lagoon a mist drifting and low had crept, erasing slowly the glittering images of the stars. . . . It flowed cold and gray in the darkness." Light temporarily dissipates the "vapor" and the shadows, restoring both darkness and sunshine as "from the black and wavy line of the forests a column of golden light shot up into the heavens." But this outcome, like the fate of Arsat, remains variable in "a world of illusions" in which white and black are interchangeable:

A white eagle rose with a slanting and ponderous flight, reached the clear sunshine and appeared dazzlingly brilliant for a moment, then soaring higher, became a dark and motionless speck before it vanished into the blue as if it had left the earth forever.

Having denied his loyalty, Arsat can no longer distinguish "the great light of a cloudless day" from "the dumb darkness." They seem equivalent:

In the merciless sunshine the whisper of unconscious life grew louder, speaking in an incomprehensible voice round the dumb darkness of that human sorrow.... "Now I can see nothing—see nothing! There is no light and no peace in the world; but there is death—death for many."

The image of light, lacking a definitive reference, has lost its clear-cut moral relevance; it has created a new "inhuman" reality in alliance with darkness.

The Nigger of the "Narcissus" (1897) brings together the diverse functions of Conrad's imagery, replicating the seamen's discord, depression, and irresolution. In passages denoting conflict or contamination, light once again gets submerged or inverted. Collisions between sound and silence repeat the collision of moral contraries, as abrasive noises overpower peaceful silence:

The resplendent and bestarred peace of the East was torn into squalid tatters by howls of rage and shrieks of lament.

Two young giants with smooth, baby faces [were] silent, and smiling placidly at the tempest of good-humored and meaningless curses.

The Russian Finn, in the racket of explosive shouts and rolling laughter, remained motionless, limp and dull, like a deaf man without a backbone.

There was a moment of surprised stillness. Then the forecastle floor disappeared under men whose bare feet flopped on the planks as they sprang clear out of their berths.

He put his hand to his side and coughed twice, a cough metallic, hollow, and tremendously loud; it resounded like two explosions in a vault.

He went on smoking in the profound silence. The wisdom of half a century spent in listening to the thunder of the waves had spoken unconsciously through his old lips. The cat purred on the windlass. Then James Wait had a fit of roaring, rattling cough that shook him, tossed him like a hurricane.

The grinding links sent through the ship a sound like a low groan of a man sighing under a burden.

"In the teeth of a screeching squall," hail "rattled on the rigging, leaped in handfuls off the yards, rebounded on the deck"; the wind makes "a terrible uproar," the sea "roaring wildly" as the "black squall howled low over the ship." The men scream or curse, then quiet down: "In all that crowd of cold and hungry men, waiting wearily for a violent death, not a voice was heard; they were mute, and in somber thoughtfulness listened to the horrible imprecations of the gale."

But soon their customary babble breaks the silence with "a rare lot of noise," a "confounded row," until, just as inevitably, the "tumult of yells rose in the light, abruptly ceased," and "the tramping noises, the confused sound of voices, died out" in deference to the captain, "the little quiet man [who] seemed to have found his taciturn serenity in the profound depths of a larger experience." The seamen constantly reverse their moods just as the sea does, and at last

> the murmur of lively talk suddenly wavered, died out, . . . the ship wrapped up in a breathless silence; a fearless ship that seemed to sleep profoundly, dreamlessly, on the bosom of the sleeping and terrible sea . . . that, stretching away on all sides, merged into the illimitable silence of all creation.

Sound and silence collide ceaselessly, neither one replacing the other permanently, never ending their contest, while the men oscillate between generosity and intolerance.

Reinforcing the auditory collisions, light collides with darkness in sharply etched combat that favors the latter:

> The main deck was dark aft, but halfway from forward, through the open doors of the forecastle, two streaks of brilliant light cut the shadow of the quiet night that lay upon the ship.

> Out of the abysmal darkness of the black cloud overhead white hail streamed on her. . . . It passed away. . . . Nothing seems left of the whole universe but darkness, clamor, fury—and the ship.
>
> On the edge of the horizon, black seas leaped up towards the glowing sun.
>
> At night, through the impenetrable darkness of earth and heaven, broad sheets of flame waved noiselessly; and for half a second the becalmed craft stood out with its masts and rigging, with every sail and every rope distinct and black in the center of a fiery outburst, like a charred ship enclosed in a globe of fire.

The imagery pictures not only this oscillation between contrary positions but also the corruption of belief. Light loses its positive identity and becomes subject to dark connotations, "sinister" rather than life-supporting, perverse, not comforting: "this unnatural and threatening daylight, in which we could see one another's wild eyes and drawn faces, was only an added tax on our endurance." Starlight, usually associated with nautical guidance, repeats the danger delivered by "ghastly" daylight:

> On the black sky the stars . . . glittered hard and cold above the uproar of the earth; they surrounded the vanquished and tormented ship on all sides: more pitiless than the eyes of a triumphant mob, and as unapproachable as the hearts of men.

But Conrad found that light associated with either good or evil was inadequate to transmit its extreme dislocation. Reaching for a metaphorical medium more suitable to an "inconclusive" drama, he called again upon a muddled mix of opposites, an indeterminate hybrid "gleaming in the murky turmoil," to gauge the crew's confusion. Belief "commingles" with rejection in a shadowy blur.

Shadows engulf the men from the outset; in the half-light that filters down to their berths, they wait passively, "lost in the gloom of those places that resembled narrow niches for coffins in a whitewashed and lighted mortuary." At roll call, each individual, "detaching himself from the shadowy mob of heads visible above the blackness of starboard bulwarks, would step barefooted into the circle of light and in two noiseless strides pass into the shadows on the port side of the quarter-deck."

The ship leaves her safe harbor in a "slight haze" as a "short black tug" intrudes on the "sunlit mist." The tugboat

> resembled an enormous and aquatic black beetle, surprised by the light, overwhelmed by the sunshine, trying to escape with ineffectual effort into the distant gloom of the land. She left a lingering smudge of smoke on the sky.

At sea, "the invisible sun, sweeping above the upright masts, made on the clouds a blurred stain of rayless light," and in a dead calm,

> the moonlight clung to [the ship] like a frosted mist. . . . And nothing in her was real, nothing was distinct and solid but the heavy shadows that filled her decks with their unceasing and noiseless stir: the shadows darker than the night and more restless than the thoughts of men.

And the immortal sea stretched away, immense and hazy, like the image of life, with a glittering surface and lightless depths.

The crewmen reach safety but not clarity: "at night the headlands retreated, the bays advanced into one unbroken line of gloom. The lights of the earth mingled with the lights of heaven." The narrator, in his Olympian fashion, recalls a "shadowy ship manned by a crew of Shades. They pass and make a sign, in a shadowy hail."

As a man of color, James Wait literally embodies the unmediated visage of identity dissolution. Shadows compose his face, a physical fusion of light and darkness, at once "pathetic and brutal," "domineering and pained." His eyes, "insolent and melancholy, . . . bulged out with an expression audacious and sad." He "held his head up in the glare of the lamp—a head vigorously modeled into deep shadows and shining lights." "The lightning gleamed in his big sad eyes that seemed in a red flicker to burn themselves out in his black face."

This visual ambivalence stumps and infects the crew: "was he a reality—or was he a sham? . . . We hesitated between pity and mistrust." Ironically a black outsider becomes "the fit emblem of their [confused] aspirations," stimulating their "humane" sympathy but also their skepticism. Hostile and deceitful yet ultimately incomprehensible—"sinister" yet vaguely worthy—he puzzles his mates with his cryptic appearance and behavior. He symbolizes and provokes in others the absence of "certitude."

The question calls for a choice between black and white, but the two colors are inextricably linked. Wait is both "bright, like the twisted flare of lightning, and more full of surprises than the dark night." Following his first appearance in a "feeble gleam," he lives in gloom, an indecipherable "mystery." His career resists objective closure; his identity is impossible for the crew to grasp because it is insubstantial, ambiguous, neither depraved nor exemplary, devoid of definite demarcation—a will-o'-the-wisp.

On his deathbed, exhausted by the debate he has initiated, he lies "stretched out black and deathlike in the dazzling light." The narrator concludes his exposition with a last judgment:

> In going he took away with himself the gloomy and solemn shadow in which our folly had posed, with humane satisfaction, as a tender arbiter of fate. And now we saw it was no such thing. It was just common foolishness. . . . Doubt survived Jimmy.

At journey's end, old Singleton, who had "never hesitated in the great light of the open sea, could hardly find the small pile of gold in the profound darkness of the shore." The momentous, "highly humanized" sympathy of his shipmates turns out to be only an "illusion of splendor and poetry." And without that collective illusion they "appeared to be creatures of another kind—lost, alone, forgetful, and doomed, . . . like mad castaways making merry in the storm and upon an insecure ledge of a treacherous rock."

The men pathetically try to regain their self-possession, their innocent generosity and trusting fellowship, at the Black Horse tavern. Metaphor suggests that they will succeed in reinstating the vitality of light, as

> a flood of sunshine streamed down the walls of grimy houses. The dark knot of seamen drifted in sunshine. . . . To the right of the dark group the stained front of the Mint,

cleansed by the flood of light, stood out for a moment dazzling and white like a marble palace in a fairy tale.

After experimenting with the convergence of contrasting images in "The Lagoon," *Almayer's Folly, An Outcast of the Islands*, and *The Nigger of the "Narcissus*," the author continued his metaphorical exploration with the remarkable technical audacity of *Heart of Darkness*. Conrad had found that light and darkness images can embody not only a systematic rivalry or a succession of contrary positions, but rather a disorderly "commingling" in a shadowy blur that mingles laudable purpose with horrific brutality.

Reaching for a vehicle suitable to depict this unspeakable paradox, he called upon the imagery he had surveyed in earlier works to gauge an unfathomable subjective condition, an indeterminate reality "gleaming in the murky turmoil," an intangible intimacy mixing the predictable with the "evanescent," a mottled mixture of "an impalpable grayness, . . . in a sickly atmosphere of tepid skepticism, without much belief." Light becomes dim, not enlightening, "unexciting" rather than victorious or overpowered or perverted, contributing a "vague" but visible presence to "one of Marlow's inconclusive experiences."

Neither sight nor insight is "very clear," the narrator exclaims: "darkness was here yesterday," but now "we live in the flicker," in the "spectral illumination of moonshine." Marlow's face, as he tells his tale, "seemed to retreat and advance out of the night in the flicker of the tiny flame" offered by a match, suspended (like Kurtz) between clarity and formlessness. Marlow pursues Kurtz to the heart of shadows—diffuse, deceptive, ever-changing, "inconclusive."

The coast of Africa and one of its murky rivers blend light and dark in a fluid fusion "blurred by a creeping mist." Ethical and emotional issues as well as physical distinctions become clouded, foggy. At a company station in the "gloomy circle of some Inferno," Marlow sees "black shapes . . . clinging to the earth, half coming out, half effaced within the dim light, . . . black shadows of disease and starvation, lying confusedly in the greenish gloom." "I didn't want any more loitering in the shade," he admits.

Everywhere he looks, reassuring principles fade into ancient irrationality; light and darkness cohabit in a "nightmarish" half-light that deranges perception and judgment while a bend in the river is "overshadowed." Moonlight, firelight, starlight, and dusk halfway reveal, halfway hide the "extravagant mystery" of cultural order comporting with primitive impulse. Gross, ghastly, indistinct shapes replace familiar, sharply etched forms, and emit indefinable fright.

Conrad took his literary expertise to its limit in *Heart of Darkness* by giving a tangible presence to "indescribable" muddle. He made self-contradiction apparent in indecisive sequences featuring exaggerated stereotypes, cacophonies of sound, and blurred phantoms that encompassed the indescribable interpenetration of light and darkness. He imagined an incredible exchange between articulate identities and the "mute" perversion that dissolves them. Marlow struggles mightily to explain but achieves only partial success in a valiant effort to evaluate the shadowy "derangement" of noble missionary purpose formerly epitomized by Kurtz.

Conrad's virtuosity culminated in his masterpiece, *Lord Jim*, probably the best novel, a superlative synthesis of satirical characterization and spectral imagery, narrative ingenuity, and rhetorical finesse—a rare balance of subjective imagination, objective fact, and discursive analysis. Three figurative usages—clear-cut competition, "unnatural" conversion, and confused intermingling—compose a literary language that collaborates with the story sequence and speech patterns. Light and dark once again not only transmit or reverse their ancient connotations, they come together in a confusing murk that distorts traditional distinctions.

Imagery, the "appalling face of things," tells the story in a variety of ways. "The sea, with its laboring waves for ever rising, sinking, and vanishing to rise again, [is] the very image of struggling mankind." A medley of abrasive and soft shipboard sounds conveys the irregular rhythm of existence:

> The patent log on the taffrail periodically rang a single tinkling stroke for every mile traversed on an errand of faith. Above the mass of sleepers a faint and patient sigh at times floated, the exhalation of a troubled dream; and short metallic clangs bursting out suddenly in the depths of the ship, the harsh scrape of a shovel, the violent slam of a furnace-door, exploded brutally, as if the men handling the mysterious things below had their breasts full of fierce anger.

The *Patna*'s rusted bulkhead mirrors the seaman's weathered endurance: "old iron can be as tough sometimes as the spirit of some men we meet now and then, worn to a shadow and breasting the weight of life." And ashore, Stein sees in his rare butterfly "an image of something as perishable and defying destruction as these delicate and lifeless tissues displaying a splendor unmarred by death."

To launch the novel, Conrad proposes a reversal of values rather than their competition or "concatenation." When the *Patna* steams toward the Red Sea, dazzling brightness, "a fulgor of sunshine," instead of signaling the promise of vitality, "killed all thought, oppressed the heart, withered all impulses of strength and energy." The sky was "viscous, stagnant, dead," and "still, hot, heavy" days fell "into an abyss" while the ship "held on her steadfast way black and smoldering in a luminous immensity, as if scorched by a flame flicked at her from a heaven without pity." Contrarily, darkness, far from appearing inhospitable, "descended on her like a benediction."

Soon, however, light and dark not only reverse their ancient connotations, they merge in disorienting shadows that obscure traditional distinctions and foment "incertitude." Day becomes indistinguishable from night as a "few dim flames in globe-lamps" cast "blurred circles of light." Conrad believed in reiteration, so his scenes emit "diffused light" in wave after wave. "A brooding gloom lay over this vast and monotonous landscape; the light fell on it as if into an abyss. The land devoured the sunshine."

Marlow repeatedly identifies that brooding gloom with his subject. "I don't know why," he says, "he should always have appeared to me symbolic . . . .. I don't know why, listening to him, I should have noted so distinctly the gradual darkening of the river, of the air, . . . effacing the outlines, burying the shapes deeper and deeper."

During a storm, identities become unrecognizable. "A straight edge of vapor lined with sickly whitish gleams flies up from the southwest, swallowing the stars in whole constellations; its shadow flies over the waters, and confounds sea and sky into one abyss of obscurity." Deepening the confusion, a lamp hardly relieved the "pitchy blackness"; Jim "saw just one yellow gleam of the masthead light high up and blurred like a last star ready to dissolve." Light was both present and absent: the masthead lamps burned through the night but "we did not see them. They were not there." "There was not a glimmer" when Jim jumped into chaos.

At dawn, as the "glitter of the sunshine" renewed his optimism, Jim realizes that "the sun could not make me mad. . . . *That* rested with me." He had not seen "the shadow of the coming event. The only shadow on the sea was the shadow of the black smoke pouring heavily from the funnel its immense streamer, whose end was constantly dissolving in the air." Daydreaming about "gorgeous virility" that possessed "the charm of vagueness," he could not forecast or prepare for his leap into an insidious alternate universe.

"Lord" Jim (an ironic title) tarnished his integrity with a jump from the *Patna,* lapsing into silence and doubt, but the urgent demand of ideal manhood persists, instigating a nebulous union with the facts of betrayal and cowardice. Formerly a prime example of confident self-knowledge, this minister's son can hardly recognize the hazy hybrid he has become. An inglorious, indefinite, indistinct identity has replaced his clear-cut conception of commendable masculine conduct.

Like Arsat and Karain, he cannot keep from resurrecting a deeply buried disgrace, a painful, humiliating misadventure that deflated his vanity. Neither a despicable coward nor an intrepid hero, he inhabits, like Conrad's most interesting characters, a no-man's land, seeking redemption in a final courageous act. Hoping to be vindicated, he cannot "submit" to the distressing mixture of mighty opposites.

But will a show of bravery extricate him from a gloomy preoccupation with squalid behavior? Can he reinstate his dedication to noble enterprise? Can he succeed in reaching a plausible conciliation or is his involvement with his dark side, the "destructive element," incurable?

After the *Patna* fiasco, shapeless furies pursue him relentlessly. At the marine hearing, the ship's shamed crewmen sat in the "half-light of the big courtroom where the audience seemed composed of staring shadows." Jim's face, once informed by great security, "unbounded safety and peace," was like "a darkening sky before a clap of thunder, shade upon shade imperceptibly coming on, the gloom growing mysteriously intense in the calm of maturing violence."

> [Jim] appealed to all sides at once—to the side turned perpetually to the light of day, and to that side of us which, like the other hemisphere of the moon, exists stealthily in perpetual darkness, with only a fearful ashy light falling at times on the edge.

Marlow takes Jim's identity to be "remarkable" yet indeterminate. Merging generality with concrete observation, he valiantly attempts to define a "disembodied spirit":

> [Jim's] imperishable reality came to me with a convincing, with an irresistible force. I saw it vividly, as though in our progress through the lofty silent rooms amongst fleeting gleams of light and the sudden revelations of human figures stealing with flickering flames within unfathomable and pellucid depths, we had approached nearer to absolute Truth, which, like Beauty itself, floats elusive, obscure, half submerged, in the silent still waters of mystery.

A thunderstorm reveals Jim's outline clearly, then indistinctly, then not at all:

> The sustained and dazzling flickers seemed to last for an unconscionable time. . . . I looked at him, distinct and black, planted solidly upon the shores of a sea of light. At the moment of greatest brilliance the darkness leaped back

with a culminating crash, and he vanished before my dazzled eyes as utterly as though he had been blown to atoms.

Marlow has no final answer to this mystery, this unspeakable interchange of light and darkness obstinately addressed by his protégé. He knows that the world of passionate idealism is filled with high-sounding abstractions that prove to be empty or illusory, a conclusion announced by many writers in the East and West, but he finds in Jim an even more puzzling outcome. He complains that "I am fated never to see him clearly," and in his last view "he passes from my eyes like a disembodied spirit astray amongst the passions of this earth, ready to surrender himself faithfully to the claim of his own world of shades."

Marlow's description of Stein, a "romantic" collector of insects, pertains to Jim equally well. Stein passes

> out of the bright circle of the lamp into the ring of fainter light—into shapeless dusk, . . . as if these few steps had carried him out of this concrete and perplexed world. His tall form, as though robbed of its substance, hovered noiselessly over invisible things with stooping and indefinite movements.

Stein too seems to be a "shadow prowling amongst the graves of butterflies." In the gloom, he speaks authoritatively about Jim's "invisible things," but in the bright light of the lamp "the austere exaltation of a certitude seen in the dusk vanished from his face. . . . The light had destroyed the assurance which had inspired him in the distant shadows."

His vision, like Jim's, circumscribes a "vast and uncertain expanse." His "dimly lit" study creates an appropriate ambiance for an "enigmatical" figure that is intense and spectral, ephemeral and unchangeable. Words written on boxes "glittered mysteriously upon a vast dimness." "Only one corner of the vast room . . . was strongly lighted by a shaded reading-lamp, and the rest of the spacious apartment melted into shapeless gloom like a cavern."

Stein had seen the Patusan natives "in the original dusk of their being"; Jim arises from his own dusk to bring light to the natives "for the sake of better morality." Like "the immovable forests," he soared "towards the sunshine" from "a shadowy and mighty tradition." He ended factional rivalry, governed wisely, and considered a coffee plantation.

But as the permanent resident of a shady, mystical realm, he cannot thrive in bright practical activity. The sun does not shine on the plantation. Instead, Marlow reports, "the yellow glow of the rising moon seemed to cast its shadow upon the ground," and in that "mournful eclipse-like light . . . the heavy shadows fell at my feet on all sides." Jim gravitates to the moonlight; its "sheen descended, cold and pale, like the ghost of dead sunlight," robbing "all forms of matter . . . of their substance, and [giving] a sinister reality to shadows alone."

Marlow's last sight of Lord Jim recaps the metamorphosis: Jim is at first "persistently visible," then starkly outlined against the darkness, then obscured and belittled, his "opportunity . . . still veiled." In the "ebbing" twilight, he "appeared no bigger than a child—then only a speck, a tiny white speck, that seemed to catch all the light left in a darkened world. . . . And suddenly, I lost him."

These shadowy observations tell a poignant story, by twilight, lamplight, starlight, and moonlight, as expressively as the urgent conversations, the intricate narrative design, and the explicit judgments by the author and his spokesmen. No wonder Conrad (in his note on "Youth") called the best years of his writing career "a period dominated by *Lord Jim*."

He painted his "largest canvas" in *Nostromo*. Light again appears to be intensely combative, or reversed in moral implication, or shifting, dappled, and dim in a shadow world. At one moment, powerful sunshine engages its eternal foe—"impenetrable darkness," "blind darkness"—in ancient debate. At the next moment, any customary association of light with health, mental balance, insight, and happiness gets displaced by its antithesis.

And then both well-defined competition and negative associations give way to gloomy uncertainty, shifting and dim in Conrad's shadow world, as the "shadow of the mountains" prevents "clear-cut vision [and] dissolves [the mountain] into great piles of gray and black vapors." Speckled shadows that mingle contrary expectations in disorganized misperception become dominant.

Two minor figures illustrate that ambiguity. Metaphor for Conrad always involved more than colorful visual allusions and striking auditory effects. Since characters defined by stereotypical qualities or values may be said to symbolize those qualities or values, they may be called "emblems," like certain objects. In the chaotic assemblage called Costaguano, Hirsch and Holroyd stand out with obvious allegorical significance in a coupling of dissimilar types. Though positioned at opposite ends of the social hierarchy, they may both be described as opportunists in a divided society, each an emblematic figure bringing together contrary values.

In the lower depths of Sulaco, the despised Jew Hirsch scrabbles for survival, while thousands of miles away, John Holroyd, a godlike millionaire, officiates over "the religion of silver" with advice and funding. Holroyd exemplifies for Gould the ultimate business genius, respectable, potent, and unreachable. Hirsch, contrarily, exemplifies for Nostromo the failed schemer, the ultimate pariah—isolated, unstable, and contemptible.

But Hirsch's corpse appears, in a gruesome, surreal episode, as Nostromo's double as well as his foil. By that time, the capataz has perceived his own status to be as moribund and inconsequential as the body of Hirsch dangling on a rope, "casting an enormous and distorted shadow upon the wall." Nostromo too has become "the shadow of a man." Infuriated by Monygham's apparent indifference to his "desperate" situation and "disarmed" by a "sense of betrayal and ruin," he sees in the grotesque dead man his own futility:

> Listening as if in a dream, [he] felt himself of as little account as the indistinct, motionless shape of the dead man whom he saw upright under the beam, with his air of listening also, disregarded, forgotten, like a terrible example of neglect.... "The capataz is undone, destroyed."... And his eyes met again the shape of the murdered man suspended in his awful immobility.

"I am nothing!" he mutters. He has changed from an illustrious hero into a secretive, fearful "scoundrel" beset (like Conrad's other muddled figures) by persistent longings for honorable identification.

But disgrace is not the last word for either Nostromo or Hirsch. Just as the Jew's defiant insult provoked a gunshot that ended unbearable torture, so does Nostromo's defiant theft of the silver—an attempt to avoid "the immobility of a disregarded man"—lead to the gunshot that ends unbearable *self*-torture. The pathetic image of "the late Señor Hirsch" conveys both the loss and restitution of "manliness," and it does so more poignantly than Conrad's voluminous thesis statements.

Holroyd, the mine's financier, is equally ambiguous. The silver, he contends, introduces "justice, industry, and peace," but also "a purer form of Christianity." For "most of the Europeans in Sulaco . . . the silver of the mine had been the emblem of a common cause, the symbol of the supreme importance of material interests." For Charles Gould, those interests would benefit the people, producing "another victory gained in the conquest of peace, . . . a serious and moral success.".

At the same time he presides over a corrupt empire. Is "the silver of the mine" the nation's savior or seducer? One image may have different connotations for different observers. Mrs. Gould, before her awareness of its darker side, observes that "the San Tomé mine was to become an institution, a rallying point for everything in the province that needed order and stability to live." Later she realizes that such an institution can also become an obsession, a "fetish [that] had grown into a monstrous and crushing weight." Decoud complains that "now the whole land is like a treasure-house, and all these people are breaking into it, while we are cutting each other's throats."

Nostromo too feels the negative impact of the silver. "An incorruptible metal that can be trusted to keep its value forever," it contains "the secret of his safety, of his influence, of his magnificence, of his power over the future, of his defiance of ill-luck." But he finds that "he had not regained his freedom. The spectre of the unlawful treasure arose, . . . [and] his soul died within him." The personification of purity embodies a suspension between greed and "incorruptible" mettle.

As shadows descend into "obscurity," the bright glow of impeccable reputation turns out to be as "illusory" as his silvery savior;

only a residue of sporadic hope and vital belief remains to counterbalance a depressing load of disillusion. Before his deliverance by an unintended gunshot, Nostromo attains affluence but loses self-respect; the legendary reputation of "the magnificent capataz de cargadores" remains as bright but as "illusory" as his silvery savior.

He will marry Linda "in the dusk and gloom of the clouded gulf . . . where [he] "stored his conquests of love and wealth." He frets that a new lighthouse "would kindle a far-reaching light upon the only secret spot of his life . . .. He saw it shining upon disgrace, poverty, contempt." "He would not go near lighted windows again," and he dies with only "the shadow of the old magnificent carelessness in his voice," his "airy soul bright and warm, like sunshine—soon clouded, and soon serene."

Similarly, the moral contradictions afflicting others have not really been reconciled. When Sulaco becomes the capitol of an independent republic, its citizens might seem to be pacified at last. After "the daybreak struggled with the gloom," the bright sun dissipates the haze of indecision and re-establishes a keen distinction between good and evil: it "precipitated the delicate, smooth, pearly grayness of light . . . into sharp-cut masses of black shade and spaces of hot, blinding glare." Recognizable categories inhabit the world once more, illuminated even at night by "the lights of the San Tomé mine, a whole mountain ablaze like a lighted palace above the dark Campo."

But imagery uncovers a distressing contradiction; the mountain's silver entails a mixed blessing. A positive connotation initially prevails in the home of the Violas as "narrow bright lines of sunlight" create a "gaily peaceful" scene. Then a rioter provokes fear in "the darkness of the room striped by threads of quiet sunlight alight with evil." Giorgio lets in a "flood of light," but "the sunshine itself was heavy and dull—heavy with pain," and Giselle shields her eyes "as if afraid to face the light." After Nostromo's confession to her, "the densest blackness of the Placid Gulf seemed to fall upon her head." Light has gone from "tranquil" to threatening, or from "resurgent" to "vanquished." "Glaring," "glittering," "brilliant" sunshine combats and is defeated by or shares in the properties of a "black gulf."

Decoud before his suicide "pulled away from the cliff of the Great Isabel, that stood behind him warm with sunshine, as if with the heat of life, bathed in a rich light from head to foot as if in a radiance of hope and joy." Yet despite the "glory" and "glitter," an ominous silence "stretched taut like a dark, thin string." Light regularly fails, "vanquished in a life-long struggle with the powers of moral darkness, whose stagnant depths breed monstrous crimes and monstrous illusions." Like darkness, it harbors disquieting fantasies.

Gould obsessively grows richer and more powerful but more "compromised." Mrs. Gould, resigned, tends to her charities without hope, "surviving alone the degradation of her young ideal of life, of love, of work." Antonia grieves for Decoud and her father, both sacrificed during the revolution. Pompous Captain Mitchell remains implacably dense; Doctor Monygham, now elevated by pretentious medical responsibilities, feels "poverty-stricken, miserable, and starved"; Viola and his daughters are spiritually paralyzed by his fatal error.

A corrupt dictatorship has given way to a more enlightened social order that nevertheless inherits perpetual difficulties brought about by grief, ignorance, injustice, avarice, frustration, and poor judgment. The integrity of the new republic will be as problematic as the fragile integrity of its leaders and ordinary citizens. And the darkness of the gulf is still "impenetrable," its shadows still secretive, a "long shaft of sunlight" only intermittent.

Twilight brings consolation as well as remorse: "the whole degradation of dignity was hidden now by the gathering dusk." "Against the moral darkness of the land," Antonia prefers "the gloom of the Los Hatos woods," and so does Conrad, immersing his actors in "a heavy black shadow in the torchlight," "the glow of a heap of charcoal," "a great recrudescence of obscurity," "a red dusk crowded with aimless dark shadows drifting in contrary directions," and "convoluted folds of gray and black."

Dappled light can offer solace: "in contrast with the white glaring room the dimly lit corridor had a restful mysteriousness of a forest shade." "The shadow of the treasure may do just as well as the substance," Monygham comments.

Conrad painted his "largest canvas" by mixing the bright glow of questionable leadership with the depressing darkness of disillusion and corruption, yielding speckled shadows that fuse the two in indefinable disorder. Apart from a regrettable excess of commentary, his command of literary resources was never better.

In "The Secret Sharer" (1912), light and dark merge once more, their conjunction transient, fortuitous, inexplicable, and yet revelatory. The narrator observes his ship drifting toward destruction, "with the great shadow gliding closer, towering higher, without a light, without a sound." Shadows seem to be submerging energy, obscuring vision, and promising annihilation.

At the same time, they unveil the emergence of a man, an indistinct but admirable progress. After unveiling the "secret" dimensions of integrity, the indeterminate images are resolved by a triumphant discursive ending ("a free man, a proud swimmer striking out for a new destiny"). The fledgling captain, seconded by his secret sharer, escapes spiritual disarray and succeeds in establishing a masculine identity acquainted with but uncontaminated by fear and insecurity.

He arrives at that position under frightful duress. Sound images develop the inward process, reinforced by rhetorical repetition and narrative progression. In contrast to "Typhoon," an "immense stillness" envelops the "test of manliness": "there was not a sound in her—and around us nothing moved, nothing lived." The story takes place during a disabling silence rather than the disabling storm that assaulted Leggatt, Captain MacWhirr, and others. The abnormal absence of sound seems "against nature, inhuman," an unwholesome quietude that threatens the ship, immobilized in a "dead calm":

> The Sunday quietness of the ship was against us; the stillness of air and water around her was against us; the elements, the men were against us—everything was against us in our secret partnership.

> Such a hush had fallen on the ship that she might have been a bark of the dead.

The resumption of sound announces the ship's deliverance ("the foreyards ran round with a great noise, amidst cheery cries"), but noise is not always positive. Leggatt had to cope with "the maddening howling of that endless gale, and on [top of] that the voice of the old man started raving like the rest of them." Nor has silence been entirely damaging. Although the narrator and his partner can converse only in "hurried whispers" or remain silent, that necessity facilitates their "communion"--"the way of silent knowledge and mute affection." Auditory allusions can be as contradictory as references to light and darkness. Like the characters they refer to, they too can signal the exhibition of paradox.

Light and dark bear multiple connotations. Occasionally they fall into simple opposition: "the riding light in the forerigging burned with a clear, untroubled, as if symbolic, flame, confident and bright in the mysterious shades of the night." But for the most part, the "troubled incertitude" of shadows, characterized by silence, solitude, and immobility, displaces such clear-cut opposition. The narrator sees his ship drifting toward destruction, "with the great shadow gliding closer, towering higher, without a light, without a sound."

Leggett, composite symbol of fallibility and strength, first appears in "the shadow of the ship's side," an "opaque belt of shadow on the darkling glassy shimmer of the sea." His "dimly pale" face and form emit "a faint flash of phosphorescent light" that "flickered" in the night sky. Once aboard, he maintains a shadowy presence, visible yet hidden, that inspires the captain until departing in gloom.

The issue raised by the fugitive is enveloped in haze: the captain endures his trial in dim solitude between the "shadow of the land" and "the shadowy water," foregoing safe seamanship to launch a brave but unpredictable venture that will prove his nautical skill or end in humiliation. A "phosphorescent flash" of the white hat he had impulsively offered Leggatt "in pity" serves "for a mark to help out the ignorance of [his own] strangeness" and deliver him from "incertitude."

In *The Shadow-Line* (1917), one of Conrad's last works, the age-old rivalry resumes, with darkness the usual winner:

> The darkness had risen around the ship like a mysterious emanation from the dumb and lonely waters.

> The only spot of light in the ship at night was that of the compass-lamps. . . . For the rest we were lost in the darkness.
>
> When the time came the blackness would overwhelm silently the bit of starlight falling upon the ship, and the end of all things would come. . . . It was like a foretaste of annihilation.
>
> I moved forward too, outside the circle of light, into the darkness that stood in front of me like a wall. In one stride I penetrated it. Such must have been the darkness before creation. . . . I was alone, every man was alone where he stood.
>
> The last gleam of light in the universe had gone, . . . and then perfect silence, joined to perfect immobility, proclaimed the yet unbroken spell of our helplessness, poised on the edge of some violent issue, lurking in the dark.

Conversion follows the subjugation of light. As in "Karain" and elsewhere, light sacrifices its usual status as beacon of hope and stability. It becomes infected, augmenting rather than dispelling the usual implications of darkness—emptiness, paralysis, isolation, menace. Intense sunlight can be as misleading, as devoid of purpose or constructive energy as total darkness, in "an empty world, steeped in an infinity of silence, through which the sunshine poured and flowed for some mysterious purpose." Both polar opposites, "white masses with dark convolutions," exert an evil influence.

Light, the beacon of hope and stability, comes to share certain negative implications of darkness—emptiness, paralysis, isolation, menace—augmenting rather than dispelling them. "There is something going on in the sky like a decomposition, like a corruption of the air," the narrator confides in his journal. Disheartened by this change, he barely manages to resist the lethal pressures exerted by moribund darkness and tainted light; he barely avoids "moral dissolution."

Disorientation, in fact, not infection or defeat, may be his chief problem; like the bewildered Arsat, the newly promoted captain cannot "see" his "enemy." An "enigmatic" convergence of contraries, first suggested in "The Lagoon," enters the already dense imagery. A shadow-line marks their intersection, "that twilight region between youth and maturity," an indefinite boundary unlike a sharply drawn battle line. It "harbors" indecision, vagueness, misperception. The rising sun turns the land into "mere dark vapor, a doubtful, massive shadow trembling in the hot glare"; the setting sun turns the land into "an ominous retreating shadow in the last gleams of twilight."

> My command seemed to stand as motionless as a model ship set on the gleams and shadows of polished marble. It was impossible to distinguish land from water in the enigmatical tranquility of the immense forces of the world.

Inscrutable scenes of hazy light, shadows, and half-lit dimness became Conrad's distinctive metaphorical signature, "emblematic" of compromised identities and unresolved outcomes. "The meaning of an episode," Conrad claimed in *Heart of Darkness*, envelops the tale like "one of these misty halos that sometimes are made visible by the spectral illumination of moonshine." As conventional techniques receded, "a shadowy country" expanded its nebulous borders, the strange linkage between light and darkness becoming more absurd and grotesque. "Indistinct" shapes achieved "a terrific suggestiveness" that sharply outlined depictions could not.

But because they were so indistinct, their impact was hard to register. "Do you see him? Do you see the story?" Conrad asks:

> Do you see anything? It seems to me I am trying to tell you a dream, . . . that commingling of absurdity, surprise, and bewilderment in a tremor of struggling revolt. . . . No, it is impossible, it is impossible to convey the life-sensation of any given epoch of one's existence—that which makes its truth, its meaning—its subtle and penetrating essence. It is impossible. We live, as we dream—alone.

Subtle implications, like Stein's elusive butterfly, may be hard to capture, but when they coalesce with an appropriate sensory carrier they can convey a disturbing reality. At times the difficulty pushed Conrad to spell out its "truth" in abstract terms. "Hate filled the world," he wrote in *Outcast*, "the hate of race, the hate of hopeless diversity, the hate of blood; the hate against the man born in the land of lies and of evil."

Such explicit formulations could not replace the immediacy of sights and sounds envisioning ambiguous actualities. Fortunately, the author moderated his addiction to generalities when he conjured the jumbled responses of characters who imagine that they are as "solid as the hills" yet show themselves to be as insubstantial as "fragments of night floating on moonbeams."

The references to light and darkness, then, project three primary story patterns—fierce competition, inexplicable conversion and fluctuation, and fluid dissolution. The first outcome reflects Darwin's biological paradox; the second, Nietzsche's concept of ethical reversal. Those patterns may conform to traditional modes of tragedy, but the third is unique. It involves the fusion of identities, not their customary rivalry or surprising inversion.

Conrad mastered the technique of distorting a "commonplace" image to form an extraordinary image that joined noble ambitions with their contradiction in a sinister, formless, dimly perceived partnership. He felt challenged to picture the internal consequence when a man of honor murders his friend or abandons his responsibility by jumping from a sinking ship. Our first president warned against political entanglement with foreign powers; Conrad imagined the psychological and moral entanglement instigated by an insidious secret sharer. His novels and tales pursued an unusual goal—to symbolize the degeneration of identity.

"Words," Marlow says, "belong to the sheltering conception of light and order which is our refuge," but words can also transmit dark derangement. Many writers have described spiritual collapse but few have attempted to distill its essence in a single "enigmatical" symbol. Moral surrender is not easy to encapsulate; the amorphous face of dissolution seems vague and unclassifiable--ugly, not elegant; disjointed, not symmetrical. It appears to be undirected, "inconclusive," subversive.

But Joseph Conrad conceived and fabricated an image that mingled sunshine with darkness to denote a fatally wounded spirit struggling in the ambiguous realm of shadows. That image stands out as his contribution to metaphorical complexity.

About the Author

Leonard Moss was born in Paterson, New Jersey in 1931, son of Pauline and Murray Moss. He attended three state universities (Oklahoma, Indiana, and California), then taught American and European literature at a fourth (SUNY Binghamton and Geneseo). At Geneseo he directed a program in comparative literature until his retirement in 1989. He did not lecture: the best part of teaching, he always said, was swapping ideas with his students. He learned as much as they did from the lively give-and-take of guided discussions.

As a Fulbright professor he chaired the English Department at the University of Athens in 1976-77 and taught graduate students at the Foreign Studies University in Beijing in 1985-87 and 1993-94. The peak years of his career were spent in China, where he met and married, after overcoming bureaucratic nonsense, Shaoping Wu, a spirited English teacher.

Professor Moss edited the journal of the Rhode Island Jewish Historical Association in Providence from 1998 to 2004. During fifty years of research and writing he wrote books on Arthur Miller, Joseph Conrad, tragedy and philosophy, Darwin and literature, imagery, and identity, completing these projects by the age of eighty-eight. "Revision is the key to vision," he would say. "I may not have the brainpower of a genius, but I am persistent."

After retirement, he enjoyed reading and writing, swimming and walking, drawing, and nurturing tomato and pepper plants. Above all, he delighted in his wife, a technology librarian at Mt. Holyoke College, and their talented son. The three were good companions and enjoyed vacationing at Cape Cod before relocating to the San Francisco Bay Area. The sea, sun, and sand, he believed, were more therapeutic than any doctor.

His grateful conclusion after a long, rewarding, sometimes arduous journey through life—"mission accomplished." On that subject, he liked a poem by Emily Dickinson, his favorite poet:

I stepped from plank to plank
A slow and cautious way,
The stars about my head I felt,
About my feet the sea.

I knew not but the next
Would be my final inch—
This gave me that precarious gait
Some call experience.

www.ingramcontent.com/pod-product-compliance
Lightning Source LLC
Chambersburg PA
CBHW070638220526
45466CB00001B/224